# AMERICA'S FIRST WORLD WAR

# AMERICA'S
# FIRST WORLD WAR

*General Pershing and the Yanks*

———— ★ ————

*by* HENRY CASTOR

*Landmark* BOOKS

RANDOM HOUSE · NEW YORK

*To the school teachers of America,*
*but especially to my well-remembered*

HANNAH R. FINGER

FRANK C. BAXTER

RUSSEL B. REYNOLDS

# Contents

AMERICA'S FIRST WORLD WAR

# 1
## Will You Work, Soldier?

John Joseph Pershing came into the world before our Civil War began. But he lived long enough to wonder about the atom bomb. History rushed onward dizzily during the long life of John Joseph Pershing.

Indeed, J.J.P. helped to hustle history along. What we call history is only a record of changes in human affairs. And J.J.P. played a leading role in many changes in military affairs. For example:

As a young fellow he dodged Indian arrows. But as an old man he had to cope with German poison gas.

Pershing always loved horses. But he became the first American general to charge into battle in an automobile.

As a green lieutenant, J.J.P. studied Apache smoke signals in New Mexico. But as a fighting general, he was the first to wire radio messages in Old Mexico.

Pershing learned jungle tracking from Philippine sultans. But he became our first high commander of airplanes in battle across the skies of France.

Last, he was the only General of the Armies of the United States. Even President Eisenhower was just one of five Generals of the *Army*. Unless laws are changed, Pershing will remain our sole General of the *Armies* forever.

And how did J.J.P.'s distinguished career begin? *By answering an ad in a newspaper!*

To begin our story at the very beginning, the first American Pershing was the General's great-grandfather. He settled in Pennsylvania in 1749.

The General's father, John Fletcher Pershing, kept a prosperous grocery store in the little village of Laclede, Missouri, when Jack was born. The birthday was September 11, 1860. The following April our North and South clashed in the awful Civil War. There is a tale that Ann Pershing had to hide her little Jack under a mattress during a raid on the Pershing store by Confederate guerrillas. The boy was less than four years old then.

The country store and their farms and children kept John and Ann busy. But John liked to take chances in life. He turned his hand to trading in real estate. Unluckily he failed and lost everything except one family farm near Laclede.

Young Jack, who was going on fourteen, was pitchforked into manhood. In the 1870s muscle power harvested most of the crops of America. A boy's muscles were valuable "farm machinery," and Jack's muscles toughened with farm work. He never grew taller than five feet ten inches, but every inch was straight up from the heels. The straight Pershing back and the powerful Pershing shoulders—as well as his chin— became his trademarks.

The folks around Laclede soon became aware of Jack's chin. When he grew angry, his jaw jutted out like a boxer's. Then also his eyes froze to a February gray, and his ordinarily mild voice cracked like a whip. Usually, however, young Jack spoke little, smiled a lot and showed deep dimples in his cheeks when he did.

Jack Pershing went to school whenever he could. The farm's chores came first. But if his education was rather hit-or-miss, his rifle marksmanship was not. The boy was a crack-shot squirrel hunter. He also learned how to ride a horse as if he and his sorrel gelding, Selim, were one. And in a curious way Jack Pershing discovered something of adult responsibilities while still in his teens. Teachers in those days did not have to have college degrees. So when the schoolmaster at a local Negro school disappeared without notice, young Jack Pershing took over the job of running his class.

Pershing invested his earnings in courses at a local normal school or teachers' college. His marks were decent in everything but vocal music. Perhaps he was like General Ulysses S. Grant in this art. Grant once said there were only two tunes he could recognize: one was *Yankee Doodle* and the other wasn't. However, if Jack Pershing could not sing worth a pail of sour cherries, he did learn to dance. And he danced exceptionally well.

At twenty-one he was still plowing, teaching and

hoping. His hopes burned to become a lawyer, and his oil lamp burned to keep his hopes warm. He read law books constantly by the light of the flickering midnight lamp.

Then came a day when one of Jack's sisters, Mary Elizabeth, showed him a newspaper. A Congressman had placed an ad in it announcing an examination to be held in St. Louis soon. Jack had no solid confidence that he could score well in the exam, but Mary Elizabeth coaxed him. She also coached him. Somewhat to his own surprise John Joseph Pershing's test score was so high that it won him the Congressman's appointment to the United States Military Academy at West Point.

His mother was quite upset. Ann Pershing had smiled and nodded when her boy declared he would become a lawyer. But to be a *soldier*—my, oh my! The very word "soldier" meant "loafer" in 1882. Civilians with bad manners sometimes chanted an insult to men in uniform: "Will you, will you, will you *work*, soldier?"

Jack soothed his mother as best he could. West Point would give him a free college education, he argued. Afterwards, when his tour of army duty was finished, he would enter law school. So his weeping

7

mother and cheering friends waved good-bye to Jack when he boarded an eastbound train.

He did not have to walk a hundred miles to the station as did one of his classmates-to-be. But Jack Pershing's own handicaps seemed stiff to him. What of his hit-or-miss schooling? What of his shaky grades? What of his country-boy inexperience? Cadet-candidate Pershing never had crossed Missouri's state lines. But now his firm chin was leading him out into the mysterious wide world.

# 2
## Indians A-Coming!

Jack Pershing's gray uniform was in apple-pie order. His brass buttons shone, his musket gleamed, his tread was steady. But Jack Pershing's heart throbbed in his throat. Plebe Cadet (freshman) Pershing was walking his first post of guard duty at West Point.

The sad-sweet notes of taps faded away. Full darkness cloaked the cliffs of West Point. The night was as hushed as the black Hudson River below. Now was the time for "ghosts of all sorts to appear from all directions," as J.J.P. wrote later.

Behold, one did! A tall spook glided toward the plebe sentry. Jack gulped and tried to remember his orders. He snapped his rifle to port-arms and challenged, "Halt! Who comes there?"

The ghost stopped still without a sound.

Jack gritted his teeth. "Halt! Who *stands* there?" he called.

The dim figure opened a folding chair and sat down, still silent. The ghost, of course, was an upperclassman testing the alertness of the plebe guard.

"Halt!" Pershing shouted. "Who *sits* there?"

J.J.P. told this story on himself twenty-five years afterward. West Point life was drudgery mixed with high jinks. Later, as an older man, J.J.P. always remembered the artillery drills with antiquated cannon, and the parades, the pillow fights, and the punishments.

He never forgot the famous Civil War generals who talked to the cadet corps. One aged officer made a deep impression on young Pershing although he never spoke at all. The old soldier was too sick. He sat huddled in blankets and watched the perfect array of the cadets pass in review. Then the old man's bearded face shone. He whispered something to his companion, Mark Twain, the famous author. The old soldier was Ulysses S. Grant.

There are likenesses between the generals, Grant and Pershing. We have already told about their tone-deafness. Besides, neither sparkled as a scholar at West Point. Both were Midwestern farm boys who went to the Point for a free college education. Neither intended to stay in the army when he could resign honorably. Both were quietly stubborn. Each was good at mathematics and as a horseman. And both won the biggest campaigns of their military careers in similar ways.

The outstanding difference between Grant and Pershing was a matter of neatness. J.J.P. always looked every inch an officer. General Grant was content to wear a shabby private's coat with buttons missing.

Perhaps Pershing was a more dogged student. J.J.P. "used to go without dinner to grind at his lessons," a friend recalled. "He was a grim scholar." Yet the cadet from Missouri had one howling fault—he lost track of time.

Often he was late for drill, for mess, for chapel. Nevertheless Jack's class voted him their "Most Soldierly Man." And the Academy's regular officers appointed him to the highest cadet rank possible every year. Pershing's tardiness hurt him in his final ratings. His grade in Discipline was only average in spite of his honor as the Most Soldierly graduate of 1886.

Brand-new Second Lieutenant Pershing picked the cavalry for his branch of service. The old horse cavalry is gone from the land today, and perhaps forever. Yet in their time the clattering riders of our army helped to win the great West. It was the U.S. Cavalry that answered the cry for help on desert and plain: "The redskins are on the warpath! Help! Indians a-coming!"

J.J.P. saw his first Indians at Fort Bayard, New Mexico, when he joined the 6th U.S. Cavalry. The lonely fort was encircled by Geronimo's Apaches. The word Apache means "enemy" and a more ferocious enemy of the white man never lived than Geronimo. This chief had slaughtered so many people by his own hand that he wore a blanket made of their scalps!

Food and ammunition ran low at Bayard. The new lieutenant, Pershing, was ordered to convoy a pack train through the hostile desert. He succeeded where others had failed at the cost of their lives. Pershing raced across 140 miles of blazing waste land in two days without losing a single man or mule.

"I had to finish the last stage of the trip on foot," he reported. "My mule was completely worn out." He had outrun the Apaches and run down his hardy mule!

Pershing was fascinated by the colorful Indians and their life. It often happens that a man learns respect for the men he fights. J.J.P. even tried to learn the Apache language when he was assigned to the Indian Scouts. These friendly army Indians were no *boy* scouts, some being in their seventies. But they were as tough as cowhide and wiser than a congress of owls. The young lieutenant learned much from them.

The Apache trouble burned out. Several years later Pershing took part in the last Indian campaign of all, the Ghost Dance War. Red tribesmen were ghost-dancing all over the West from Nevada to the Dakotas.

Lieutenant Pershing rode into South Dakota with the 6th Cavalry to be baptized by bullets and arrows. The Ghost Dance madness had infected the Sioux. This Indian nation had wiped out General Custer's 7th Cavalry fourteen years before. Now a new regiment of the 7th was pursuing a band of Sioux under Chief Big Foot.

Big Foot's people were massacred to avenge General Custer. Fortunately J.J.P. missed the butchery at Wounded Knee Creek. His troop of the 6th Cavalry was fired on at Little Grass Creek four days later. The skirmish was trifling. But the date shone for Second Lieutenant John Joseph Pershing. His first battle had been fought on the first day of the first month of 1891.

# 3

# Hay Foot, Straw Foot

In the autumn of 1891 a weather-beaten officer caught a train to Lincoln, Nebraska. Lieutenant Pershing had orders to take command of the cadet battalion at the state university. The change was a strange one for an officer who had been chasing wild Indians. Now he would be chasing wild college boys.

Many would be young farmers who didn't know their right feet from their left. "Hay foot, straw foot" was a sarcastic chant for awkward squads on the drill field in those days. The theory was that you could make a farmer understand which foot was which by naming them after something he knew. Any farm boy could tell the difference between hay and straw even if he didn't know right from left.

Pershing taught mathematics at the University of Nebraska, too. One of his students was a bright-eyed little girl of twelve whose father, James Canfield, was Chancellor of the University. Mr. Canfield had arranged courses for students who lacked high-school credits. His daughter Dorothy remembers Lieutenant Pershing's teaching. (Later in life Dorothy Canfield Fisher became one of America's distinguished writers. Among her many books are two LANDMARK BOOKS.)

"Pershing was harsh, but always fair," she says. "He stuck strictly to the textbook. He assigned work and saw that we did it. When he snapped out a question, he expected a snappy answer. John Pershing believed that geometry could be taught exactly as he taught rifle marksmanship. We younger children often were lost in the woods in Pershing's class."

Out on the drill field the Lieut, as the students dubbed him, was much more at home. Indeed, Pershing turned "hay foot, straw foot" into a hot foot! It was a resounding personal triumph because military training was dreary in 1891. The college boys couldn't be bothered—why get worked up when there never would be another war? While a West Point cadet, Pershing himself had said, "There won't be a gun fired in the next hundred years." The attitude of the Nebraska boys was no exception to the general indifference.

Yet in one short year the battalion became a keen campus activity. At the end of Pershing's four years at Nebraska the farmer-cadets were the second best corps in the United States. Only the West Pointers were better by the War Department's official rating.

How did the Lieut do it?

"Every person should do every day the thing he must do," he believed, "and should do it to the best of his ability."

There is nothing brilliant or startling about that statement. But to the Lieut it was the only way a man could live and be proud.

His spirit infected the plowboys of Nebraska. After all, the Lieut had been a plowboy too. But, despite it —didn't he look like the perfect soldier? The students began to imitate Pershing's straight-backed walk.

17

They tried to earn words of praise from him. Soon they were winning not only his praise but also every intercollegiate drill and rifle competition in sight.

When he left Nebraska, the boys requested a pair of their Lieut's cavalry trousers. They cut them up into service ribbons, dozens of small blue and gold ribbons. They were proud to call themselves "The Pershing Rifles."

Even the university girls admired the handsome officer with the ramrod spine. Especially when they discovered that he could dance beautifully!

James Canfield persuaded Pershing to enter the University law school. Both men were happy when the day came for the army officer to step onto a platform to receive his diploma. At last Pershing was the lawyer his mother always had wanted him to be.

But, lawyer or no lawyer, J.J.P. was still just a Lieut. He was thirty-five years old when he left Nebraska and never had been promoted. Nobody called him "Jack" any more. "Jack" seemed too free and easy for a middle-aged officer of J.J.P.'s stiff dignity.

Drilling the cadets, teaching math and studying law kept Pershing on the jump. He planned his working schedule on split-second timing. A funny episode happened one day that throws light on the character

of this "most soldierly" man. Dorothy Canfield tells the
story:

In his law classes J.J.P. wore civilian clothes, but
for drill he changed to uniform. Just off the parade
ground was a tent where he made very quick changes.
Law Student Pershing would rush into the tent; the
Lieut would march out seconds later.

Often he was late. One day, when he hurried into
his tent, the cadets were lined up to pass in review.
Their band was playing. People from the town who enjoyed the crisp marching of the corps were gathered to
watch. Little Dorothy Canfield was one of these spectators.

The cadet adjutant called the corps to attention
when he saw the square-shouldered Lieut leave his
tent. J.J.P. strode forward to face the cadet officer. The
adjutant swept his sword hilt up to his lips in the cus-
tomary salute. But he choked on the words he was
supposed to say. Pershing automatically brought his
hand to his forehead to return the salute. But his fin-
gertips did not touch the visor of an army officer's cap.
They felt the brim of a round, black derby hat!

J.J.P. had hurried too fast. He was facing his cadets
as an army officer from the neck down but as a law
student from the neck up.

19

He spoke not a word. Like a clockwork soldier, he about faced. Back into his tent Pershing strode, *click, click, click*. Not a man in the ranks laughed. But among the spectators little Miss Canfield giggled and giggled!

A half moment later the Lieut reappeared, *click, click, click*. He snapped his hand up in salute to the adjutant. This time his fingers touched the visor of a correct military cap.

"Pass the battalion in review," J.J.P. commanded.

His face never moved a muscle. And there was something so sober about Pershing that nobody teased him afterward. The boys must have snickered among themselves. But their Lieut's reserved manner prevented them from joshing him.

We can guess how J.J.P. reasoned out his mistake. "By the numbers," now—army style!

1. The Infantry Drill Regulations—the IDR—said nothing about wearing derby hats on parade.

2. The IDR forbade laughing on parade.

3. The IDR required a complete uniform.

4. He was not in complete uniform.

5. He had promptly gotten into complete uniform.

6. Episode—DIS-MISSED!

# 4
# Strong Chin Meets Big Teeth

When the Lieut said good-bye to his college boys, he went back to Indian country. This time he rode with the 10th Cavalry which in those days was an all-Negro regiment with white officers. The men of the 10th were fine horsemen, J.J.P. discovered. He helped them round up a slippery band of runaway Cree Indians near the Canadian border in Montana.

21

In 1896 Pershing left Montana to serve as aide-de-camp to General Nelson Miles in Washington.

General Miles had met Jack Pershing during the Apache campaign. He remembered him as the officer who had worn out a mule while outracing Geronimo. As Miles' aide in our capital, Pershing met somebody who was to raise him to the stars. This man was Theodore Roosevelt, who then was Assistant Secretary of the Navy.

Teddy Roosevelt's big teeth gleamed with pleasure when he heard about Pershing's Indian experiences. Soon T.R. was talking about his own adventures in the Wild West that he loved. Once he'd helped to arrest cattle rustlers in the Dakotas, and he could show a photograph to prove it. Had Pershing ever roped a steer? Had he disarmed a gun fighter? Had he done this, or that? T.R. talked on about cowboys and Indians and had a fine time. Pershing listened and smiled. Five years later when T.R. was President of the United States he remembered the strong-chinned lieutenant with whom he had chatted.

In the fall of 1897 J.J.P. returned to West Point to teach military tactics to new cadets. Some of the tricks he knew were not in the books. Pershing had soaked up fresh learning from his clashes with Apaches, Sioux and Crees. And maybe even from those other wild men, the Nebraska cadets.

He was chalking battle diagrams on blackboards when our battleship, the *U.S.S. Maine*, blew up in the harbor of Havana, Cuba. Almost overnight the United States whooped into war with the Spanish Empire. J.J.P. was sick of blackboards. He wanted to blow chalk dust from his nostrils and smell gunpowder again. His request to rejoin the 10th Cavalry was granted. The 10th sailed for Cuba.

The climax of the Cuban campaign was the Battle of San Juan Hill. Pershing and the troopers of the 10th Cavalry covered themselves with blood and glory on the hill. Colonel Teddy Roosevelt stole the headlines, but the Negroes of the 9th and 10th regular cavalry regiments went all the bitter way to the crest beside Teddy's Rough Riders. John Joseph Pershing won a promotion at last, from second to first lieutenant. He also won two commendations for valor. His regimental commander called J.J.P. "the coolest man under fire I ever saw."

The Spanish-American War left the United States with orphans on its hands. They were the islands of Cuba, Puerto Rico, Guam, Wake and the Philippines. Some of these waifs were overjoyed to be orphans.

They had hated Mother Spain. Nevertheless, Stepmother America had to raise them decently even if they hated her too.

A frantic War Department began to wonder which of their men could nurse orphan islands. Ah!—Lieutenant Pershing might be one. He had been a teacher as well as a fighter. He seemed to understand red-skinned and black-skinned peoples. Also he had a law degree, an unusual accomplishment for a line officer. And although he was only a first lieutenant he was a mature, sensible man. Pershing became head nurse of the infant bureau. Later it was called the Bureau of Insular Affairs.

J.J.P. soon got fed up with his desk work. He was excited when new orders relieved him. Soon he boarded a ship to sail to the Philippines, the mysterious islands that had become possessions of our nation.

# 5

## Moros, Marriage, and a Star

At the start of the present century very few Americans knew much about the Far East. We were puzzled when the people of the Philippines clawed us tooth and nail in 1899. But from the Filipinos' point of view there was nothing strange about their revolt. Yankees or Spaniards, what was the difference? Both were arrogant, unwelcome white masters to a Filipino.

Lieutenant Pershing's first two years in the Orient

were learning years. He was stationed on the Philippine island of Mindanao which is the home of the Moros. They are a slightly-built brown people who worship Mohammed. Their religion gave the devout Moro warriors an extra reason to hate Christian foreigners.

Moro swordsmen became Pershing's quarry in 1902. He had been promoted again and had pinned on the double silver bars of a captain. J.J.P.'s prowls through the mountainous jungle earned him the grudging respect of the Moros. During his learning years he had studied their language and habits. He was clever, relentless, but utterly honorable. He fought hard but never broke his word to a *datto* (chief) once he had given it. Some of the dattos called J.J.P. "the Big Datto."

Pershing's work came to the attention of the governor of the Philippines, William Howard Taft, who later became our twenty-seventh President. Governor Taft praised the new Captain in a letter to *his* President. This was none other than Theodore Roosevelt— Teddy—T.R.—"Big Teeth."

Big Teeth applauded Strong Chin in a message to Congress. This was an unusual honor for Captain Pershing, particularly when no general got such attention.

But T.R. had plans for the Captain. He called him back to Washington in 1903 to study at the War College and to help reorganize the War Department.

Desk work always made Pershing restless. However, Washington nights were full of star dust and roses this time. Captain Pershing fell in love. The girl was Frances Warren, daughter of a Senator from Wyoming. When they were married, the lovers took a honeymoon trip to Japan. There the groom had to leave his bride for a while. President Roosevelt wanted Pershing to go to Manchuria to observe the fighting between the Russians and Japanese.

Then, just before Captain and Mrs. Pershing returned to Washington in 1906, a star fell on Pershing— a general's star. He became Brigadier General John Joseph Pershing. Up from captain to general in one leap! He skipped the in-between ranks of major, lieutenant colonel and colonel. The promotion is unique in our history.

It was T.R.'s doing. Big Teeth scorned tradition if he wanted to. He thought Strong Chin was good enough to be jumped over the heads of 862 senior officers.

Pershing pinned on the star of his rank. He made a brief trip to Europe before he steamed back to the Philippines. The shy grocer's son from Laclede was becoming a seasoned globetrotter. In the Islands once more he took command of mopping up the wild Moros. Off and on for eleven years J.J.P. had conquered the dattos and sultans one by one. This was an accomplishment that the Spaniards had not been able to bring about in three hundred years.

J.J.P.'s most spectacular feat was so bold that it bordered on rashness. The General in person led some of his men in a charge on a Moro fort. Up a mountain they went, across a moat and over a wall of sharp bamboo spears. Their final rush took them headlong, bayonet first, down into the crater of a dead volcano! Pershing was recommended for the Medal of Honor for his daring at Mount Bogsak. But oddly enough he himself threw cold water on the suggestion.

"I was in that part of the line," he wrote to his superiors, "simply because my presence there was necessary." In other words: why accept a medal merely for doing one's plain duty?

What do you think the fierce Moros thought of their conqueror? Well, one sultan made Pershing a real datto; another became his blood brother in a solemn ceremony; and a third offered his son to J.J.P. The Moro said that "the American sultan" would make a splendid father for the boy.

28

But J.J.P. needed nobody else's children to raise. By now he had four of his own. When orders came in 1913 transferring him to the Presidio of San Francisco, the General was very happy. At last! A chance to be a home-body father to his three little girls and one little boy.

Probably the General hummed a gay tune—off key, of course—when he sailed away for the Golden Gate and home, sweet home.

# 6

## A Bandit Called Dorothy

Latin America, like China, has been the arena for dozens of wars. In 1913 the war god was raging in Mexico. American citizens trapped there were beaten, imprisoned and sometimes murdered. Our flag was trampled by angry and confused mobs. Finally in the spring of 1914 some American sailors were cruelly manhandled and jailed at Tampico.

President Woodrow Wilson's patience ran out. Wilson was a scholar rather than a fighter; he once had been a professor and then president of Princeton University. He ordered our Atlantic Fleet into the Gulf of Mexico. Our marines landed and seized the port of Vera Cruz. We stood at the brink of war with Mexico, our neighbor to the south.

Then onto the scene galloped a man named Doroteo Arango. (In Spanish Doroteo is the male form of the name Dorothy.) But everybody knew Arango under his alias of "Pancho Villa." For a man called Dorothy he was one of the toughest opponents American troops ever have faced. To many Mexicans he was a patriot, but to our State Department he was a mere bandit.

Pancho raided Texas. He killed Americans on American soil. War might have followed in America except that Europe went to war first. President Wilson was in a tight corner. He wanted to punish Pancho Villa— but how? With war spreading in Europe, we could not afford to become involved in a little war over here. We were desperately unprepared for almost any kind of war, large or small.

General Pershing's stay in San Francisco had been woefully short. In the summer of 1914 he was ordered to El Paso, Texas, to keep an eye on the uneasy Mexican border. The old horseman felt at home there at Fort Bliss. He had a reunion with his Negro saddle mates of the 10th Cavalry. After inspecting his regiments J.J.P. wired Washington, "I am ready to take the field on five minutes' notice."

But Pershing got an entirely unexpected notice in August, 1915. A fire broke out in the beautiful Presidio of San Francisco. The pleasant home of Mrs. Pershing and her children proved to be a death trap. Only six-year-old Warren escaped the flames that killed his mother and his three little sisters.

If you ever have lost one dear person in your own family, you know how General Pershing felt. Overnight his whole family, save one, had been taken from him without a chance to say good-bye. The marks of deep sorrow remained with the General. He never married again. His ramrod spine and his granite chin still offered quiet challenge to the world. But laughter became a rare thing for John Joseph Pershing. Most of the photographs taken of J.J.P. after 1915 show a serious face. The few laughing ones seem to have a common reason. Pershing either is holding a child in his arms or is bending down to talk to one.

The grieving General probably welcomed orders to go after wily Pancho Villa. On March 15, 1916, Pershing crossed the Rio Grande with his Mexican

Expedition—10,000 cavalry troops and the 1st Aero Squadron.

Pershing's eight flimsy Curtiss biplanes (double-winged aircraft) were the grandfathers of our great Air Force of today. The General also packed along a wireless set to keep in touch with Washington. This was the beginning of American military radio in combat. And J.J.P. rode in a topless automobile while his troopers used motor trucks. It was the first time this ever had been done in a military campaign.

Pershing was in a ticklish position. His duty was both military and diplomatic. He had to coöperate with the Mexican Federal army. His orders told him to punish Pancho Villa but did not say how. Besides, his supply line was shaky. The Quartermaster Corps trucks broke down in the rocky, roadless deserts of Chihuahua. As a result, the army mules were given the job of transporting the Expedition's supplies.

Oh, Pancho could be chased, all right. But Pancho wasn't likely to be caught. For one thing, he knew every inch of his territory. For another, he had spies everywhere, even with Pershing's guides. Pancho dodged about and laughed at the sweating, frustrated *gringo* (American) cavalry. An old border scout once said to Pershing, "Sir, it looks to me like we got Pancho Villa entirely surrounded—on one side."

The General winced. "Yes, it's like trying to catch a rat in a corn field," he said.

The Expedition fought only two minor skirmishes. Both were ambushes and cost a few American lives.

However, in spite of never capturing Pancho, the Expedition did its job. Villa's band had to disperse to avoid capture. After eleven months of dust, heat, cactus, snakes and fever, Pershing rode back to Texas.

He became Major General John Joseph Pershing, put a second star on his shoulders, and took command of the southern department of the army at San Antonio.

At about the time J.J.P. took over his new job, the world was electrified by a message out of Washington, D.C. On April 6, 1917, the United States broke off relations with the government of His Imperial German Majesty, Kaiser Wilhelm III.

# 7

## Safe for Democracy

For four years Europe had been embroiled in what we have come to call World War I to distinguish it from the later conflict we call World War II.

According to one historian the first World War grew out of "fear, hunger and pride." Certainly the world of 1914 had plenty of each.

France feared and hated Germany, who had beaten her badly in 1870. Great Britain was afraid the militant Germans would snatch away British trade and colonies. In their empire the Austrians bullied such minorities as the Czechs and the Slovaks. The Balkan nations—Serbia, Montenegro, Romania, Bulgaria, Albania and Greece—distrusted one another. But the Balkans all united in hating Austria and Turkey. The Russians called the Balkans "little brothers" and bickered with Germany, Austria and Turkey. The Turks had hated and feared the Russians for centuries. Bloated with hungry, growing populations, Italy and Japan wanted to seize territory so they could spread out.

The poor old globe seemed like a bomb waiting for someone to light its fuse!

On June 8, 1914, the match was struck, and the fuse began to sputter. On that day a terrorist killed the heir to the Austrian throne, Archduke Franz Ferdinand, and his wife during their visit to a town full of hot-headed Austria-haters. Austria-Hungary blamed its neighbors, the Serbs, for provoking the murders. One month to the day after the assassinations, Austria-Hungary attacked Serbia. You will not find either of these kingdoms on the map today. These nations vanished and new ones have appeared as a result of the great conflict.

Immediately after the attack, neutral countries tried to halt the Austrian invasion.

The Czar of Russia mobilized his troops to encourage the Serbs. The Kaiser of Germany told the Czar to cease threatening Austria, which was a partner of Germany.

France and England joined in the clamorous name calling. In fact, no ruler in Europe was willing to tone down his voice and speak softly. Everybody raved; nobody listened.

The United States wanted no part of Europe's war. We were opening the brand-new Panama Canal; we were prospering; and the foreigners' war was none of our business anyhow. Besides, we were having trouble with Mexico. Our marines had landed in Vera Cruz, and Pershing's cavalry was poised on the Rio Grande. This was war enough for President Wilson. So he told Europe that we were "too proud to fight."

Wilson's phrase stung former President Theodore Roosevelt. He called President Wilson "a spineless rabbit." *What* Americans were too proud to fight? "Professional pacifists, flub-dubs, and mollycoddles!" bellowed T.R. "That's who!"

The bitterness between these two great statesmen shows how divided the people of the United States were. In 1916 player pianos and phonographs were grinding out a popular tune, "I Didn't Raise My Boy to Be a Soldier." And peace-loving people were growing nervous when President Wilson said the nations allied against Germany and Austria were "fighting our fight." This sounded as though Wilson was preparing to take some share in the conflict.

But mere sympathy could not satisfy a tom-tom beater like Theodore Roosevelt—he wanted *action!* On the other hand our Secretary of State, William Jennings Bryan, quit the Cabinet because he felt our President was becoming *too* warlike!

The year 1915 saw a sudden change when the British ship *Lusitania* was sunk in the Atlantic. A German submarine shot a torpedo into the great liner off the coast of Ireland. The *Lusitania* plunged to the bottom of the icy ocean; and 1,200 helpless men, women and children drowned. Among them were 128 Americans.

This was dirty fighting that anybody could understand. A gale of rage shrieked across our land, and most Americans turned against Germany. The German Kaiser hastened to promise that his submarine captains would be more careful in the future. But anti-German sentiment stiffened in the United States. The

Kaiser's cause never recovered from the memory of the *Lusitania.*

In honesty we must admit that the Kaiser was in a nasty predicament. The mighty British Navy had blocked off all ships and supplies from his ports. Munitions and food poured into the harbors of Germany's foes. The Kaiser tried to choke off the flow, but the British fleet forced the Germans to use two extreme methods. One was to destroy the Allies' ships at sea by submarine warfare. The other was to destroy the Allies' factories at home by undercover agents who could sabotage vital machinery.

Both the submarine and sabotage are ugly tools of war. And Allied propaganda experts spared no labors to make the Germans look hideous. Newspapers carried tales of Belgian babies being used for Hun bayonet practice. Cartoons showed the Boche crucifying Canadian soldiers and torturing English nurses. ("Hun" and "Boche" were nasty words of the day meaning Germans.) Most of these so-called atrocity stories were imaginary. But Americans were ready to believe anything foul about a nation whose submarines sank unarmed passenger ships without warning.

Aside from the lies about the Germans, there were

real reasons for us to dislike them. Their diplomats sneered at an honest peace treaty, calling it "a scrap of paper." Their professors hailed German *kultur* as if no other nation had any culture. Their generals boasted that German troops could slice through any army in the world "like a knife through cheese." Their admirals thundered that submarine *schrecklichkeit* (frightfulness) would win the war by paralyzing their enemies with fear.

Such rude bragging irritated Americans. And on top of these minor rubs we caught the Germans red-handed in treachery. Their embassy in Washington was a nest of spies. German saboteurs blew up bridges between the United States and Canada. They hid time bombs in the coal bunkers of ships anchored in American harbors.

The Imperial German Embassy itself was trapped in a piece of skullduggery that was both stupid and astonishing. Its Minister, Alfred Zimmerman, wrote to Mexico urging that country to join with Japan in an attack on the United States. For her reward Mexico would get Texas, Arizona and New Mexico. The sensational disclosure of the Zimmerman Note proved that German scheming—idiotic as much of it was—

had something to do with Pershing's troubles below the Rio Grande.

In January, 1917, President Wilson offered his services as a neutral for the last time in hope of ending the war. But all the belligerents scorned Wilson's idea of "peace without victory." Later the same month the Kaiser commanded his submarines to carry on again their program of *schrecklichkeit*. They must sink any ship whatever that entered the war zone and shoot without warning. Any ship included American ships, of course.

Our President tried a last forlorn measure. He called on the German people to overthrow their Kaiser and his autocracy, or royal dictatorship. A section of the German Parliament agreed with President Wilson. But these few brave Social Democrats were crushingly defeated. If America wanted war she could have it, the German government said. "Wilson will bite granite!"

On April 6, 1917, the United States declared war.

"God helping her, she can do no other," spoke Woodrow Wilson. "The world must be made safe for democracy."

# 8

## Keep the Home Fires Burning

Newspaper headlines of April 6, 1917, shouted WAR! at one hundred million Americans. That is a population less than two-thirds of ours today. Their way of life was very different from ours today.

In the first place, no American home had a radio, a television set or an electric washing machine. Few indeed had telephones. In the cities gas lights outnumbered electric ones; on the farms kerosene lamps were used. If there was a record player, it ran on springs like a clock. Grownups loved to play Victor Herbert's songs on the victrola, but the kids preferred ragtime. The youngsters jigged to tunes like "Everybody's Doin' It" ("Doin' what? Turkey trot!"). One ragtime number from 1917 we still hear today is "Tiger Rag." Ragtime was the granddaddy of modern jazz.

When children could beg nickels from their parents on Saturday afternoons, they would go to the movies. The films were silent. Messages flashed on the screen to tell what the actors were saying. A piano player in the theater would bang out music to describe home-sickness, joy, fear or even a storm at sea. Women's hats were so big that sitting behind one was like sitting be-hind a bush. So the theaters slid signs across their screens reading, "Ladies Will Kindly Remove Their Hats." This was a job. The ladies used to spear their hats to their unbobbed hair with pins a foot long.

Women wore long, full skirts, but almost overnight World War I changed that ancient custom. Our Navy needed wool for uniforms, and wool was scarce. A Harvard University professor told the French Ambas-sador how he could save wool for American sailors and French soldiers. How? By telling your Paris style ex-perts to design smaller skirts, said the Professor. The

Frenchman cabled the idea to Paris. Soon women throughout the world began to wear tight or hobble skirts and later wore short ones. American sailors went to sea in trousers that had been saved from being made into skirts.

City streets and country roads were quiet. Horses pulled wagons that carried most of the traffic load. But times were changing. Nearly two million automobiles hit the roads in 1917 and, of course, began hitting one another. There were no automatic traffic signals, no white center lines and few drivers' examinations. Old-style cars ran noisily by alcohol, benzine, and steam, as well as on low-grade gasoline. They broke down frequently, and small boys would scream, "Get a horse!" General Pershing's trucks in Mexico broke down, and he had to fall back on his mules.

Almost without knowing how, the United States had become a place of big factories, big cities and big problems. By 1917 the Union as we know it today was complete; the forty-seventh and forty-eighth states, New Mexico and Arizona, had been admitted in 1912. But as our country grew, it ached with growing pains. Some were caused by waves of immigration from Europe, some by industrial troubles and some by the need for political reforms. Two reforms that were quite new in 1917 were the use of the secret ballot and the direct election of the United States Senate by the people. But in that day "the people" did not include women, for women could not vote except in a few states.

Certain special effects of World War I appeared as 1917 rolled along. Enemy foreigners were forced to register with our government. Germans were the largest foreign group of any in our land. The U.S. Attorney General told them not to fear, but he used curious words: "Just obey the law and keep your mouth shut."

Billboards splashed army and navy recruiting posters far and wide. Some declared, "Uncle Sam needs YOU!" and some, "Don't Read American History— MAKE IT!" Uncle Sam's pointing finger seemed to jump right out of those posters and follow you down the street. Sometimes he was urging his citizens to buy Liberty Bonds as well. Smaller posters in the schools coaxed children to buy twenty-five cent War Savings Stamps. And one odd poster even read, "Eat More Fish!" This was a project of the Food Administrator, Herbert Hoover, a young engineer who later became our thirty-first President. He prophesied that "Food Will Win the War." So meatless days and sugarless days became proofs of a family's patriotism.

Yet in spite of "Hooverizing," the prices of food shot up. Milk soared to a dime a quart. This frightened parents with small children because many fathers with good jobs earned only five dollars a day.

As autumn drew close and days darkened earlier, there was talk of trying "daylight saving time." Congress voted to begin it in the spring. Some people wrote letters to their papers complaining that tinkering with the hands of a clock was unholy—or at least, that the cows and chickens would be horribly confused.

During the winter school children learned how to knit. Girls made socks, boys made squares of brown wool. These squares were supposed to be sewed into blankets for our soldiers.

All of our knitting and Hooverizing and Liberty Bond buying proved clearly that we were behind our Army and Navy. One popular song told of American soldiers going "Over There." Another one said they wanted the home folks to "Keep the Home Fires Burning."

# 9

## Luxuries, Toys and Mother

At one time battle was a sporting event, a test of manhood. Warriors marched forth and banged one another with clubs. Battle was a game any number of willing amateurs could play. As time went by, warriors added horses, swords and bows and arrows to their playthings. Battles grew bigger and more expensive. In Roman times the warrior became a soldier, meaning a man who fights for pay.

By 1914 the price of losing your temper as a nation had zoomed to the skies. Every German soldier we killed in 1918 cost the United States $25,000. Today the price tag on enemies has soared out of sight both in blood and in treasure.

Six costly weapons came of age during World War I: the machine gun, the tank, the automobile, the submarine, poison gas and the airplane.

The machine gun was a dream of military mechanics as far back as ancient China. During our Civil War a loyal Southerner invented a machine gun. But Abraham Lincoln's generals spurned Mr. Gatling's gun.

Fifty years ticked by. Then the German Kaiser's army jolted the world with a sinister *rat-tat-tat-tat*. The Germans were using a machine gun of Anglo-American origin. Thus many British troops were killed by machine guns their own people had manufactured.

Hiram Stevens Maxim was the Maine Yankee who perfected his invention in England in 1889. His weapon made a three-man gun crew the equal of sixty riflemen. When the British marched into battle in 1914, their divisions carried only two machine guns apiece. Their foes, the Germans, used fifty guns apiece. However, the British commander wasn't worried—machine guns were "luxuries," he said.

48

When the Germans squeezed the triggers of their Maxim guns, they mowed down lines of young Englishmen like hay. The startled British (and the French, too) quickly adopted more "luxuries" themselves and began to chop down rank after rank of young Germans. The machine gun, behind barbed wire barriers, became king of the battlefield.

The only way to avoid its deadly touch was to go underground. So the soldiers on both sides scooped out foxholes with their bayonets or with mess kits or even with their bare hands. They linked the holes into ditches and then dug them deeper. *Within seven months the ditches became a highly complicated trench system 500 miles long.* Until then trench warfare on such a huge scale had been unknown in man's bloody history. A new phrase meaning *attack!* burst on the world: "Over the top!"

And thousands of young men walked to their death by going over the top of the trenches against hidden machine guns.

The tank threatened to crack the German machine-gun wall in 1917. Again, here was a weapon based on an old idea. But armor had disappeared from the battlefield since the days of knighthood and jousting. It remained for some Englishmen, including young Winston Churchill, to revive the idea. To keep the nature of the new machine of war a secret, the British nicknamed it a "tank." No spy could suspect anything so harmless as a *tank!* And the first useful tank bore the even more harmless name of "Mother."

The first reasonably successful use of tanks came in the gloomy sunrise of November 20, 1917. The British cranked up Mother and 377 of her sisters. They waddled straight toward the Germans across the muddy fields of Flanders near the town of Cambrai. The enemy was dumbfounded. Here came iron monsters crunching through barbed wire and spitting lead! Machine-gun bullets merely bounced off the iron-clad creatures. Many Germans ran for their lives as if they had seen invaders from Mars. The British themselves were so amazed at the unexpected success of "Mother" and her girls that they failed to take advantage of the Germans' fright.

The automobile chugged into the war dramatically. In 1914 the enemy surge into France had swept up to the very bridges of Paris itself. Along the banks of the River Marne the spike-helmeted infantry of the Kaiser gathered to capture the French capital. The French *poilus* prepared "to die in their tracks rather than retreat." *Poilu* means "hairy one." It was a pet word for the whiskery French soldiers.

Suddenly their commander, Marshal Joffre, heard hopeful news. An airplane scout reported that the right wing of the Germans was exposed to counterattack from Paris. *C'est bon,* the Marshal thought—but how to speed soldiers from the city's garrison in time? *Ah!—Les taxiautos!* Joffre piled thousands of his *poilus* into the taxicabs of Paris. They honked to the front and fell on the flank of the onrushing enemy. The German advance faltered and ground to a halt. Paris was saved! *Vive la France! Vive les taxi-autos!*

The submarine, unlike the automobile, has no peaceful uses. It is purely an engine of death. Robert Fulton built one for Napoleon even before he built his famous steamboat, the *Clermont*. The first modern submarine was designed by an American, John Holland, in 1900.

The alert Germans seized upon this Yankee invention as they had seized upon the machine gun. The Kaiser's fleet was no match for the British on the surface of the seas, and the German admirals knew this. But under the water might lie the path to victory.

They concentrated on the building of *unterseeboots,* or undersea boats, called "U-boats" for short.

These German U-boats gave the fleets of the Allies a dreadful beating. In fact, ships were sunk much faster than they could be built. One of every four British merchantmen never came home to port. And, as a bitter joke, it is possible that some of the U-boats that sent Americans to their death in the salt sea may have been American-made.

Poison gas was known to the Greeks of olden time, but German chemical skill brought it up to date. In 1915 the Kaiser's men clumsily began chemical warfare. They opened bottles of chlorine against the Algerians and Canadians in trenches near Ypres in Belgium. A green, choking cloud drifted down the wind and routed the French Algerians, but somehow the Canadians were able to hang on. The enemy did not follow up with a heavy attack, probably because they did not know how to prevent their own men from being gassed.

But once a start was made, gas became a regular weapon on both sides. Chlorine, mustard and phosphorus rotted away human lungs and burned flesh to the bone. Gas caused more American casualties than any other German weapon. Part of the reason was that many Yanks thought their gas masks were handy pouches for doughnuts and chocolate bars. So, when the signal gongs clanged to warn of a gas attack our boys had their breathing clogged by groceries.

The airplane surely was the most important new experiment of all. None of the nations clutched in a death grip in 1914 had any idea of the uses of planes. Even Marshal Joffre, who partly owed his triumph at the Battle of the Marne to an airplane scout, called airplanes "toys." This was a natural blindness, for the airplane was only eleven years old in 1914.

During the first year of World War I, planes were simply sky scouts. Now and then a pilot like the German Max Immelmann took aloft a basketful of hand grenades to throw down for fun. Once he dropped a note on Paris demanding that the city surrender to him. Max's impudence enraged the Parisians. They boiled into the streets to pop away at his little plane, even with short-range revolvers. They never touched Max, but they felt better for their shooting.

Bombing never became important despite the start Lieutenant Immelmann gave it. London suffered some raids from Gotha bombers and Zeppelins. But the damage was minor compared to the fearful ruin heaped on London and Berlin during World War II a generation later. Zeppelins were big, rigid, cigar-shaped balloons full of hydrogen gas. Few survived the war because they blew up when a flaming bullet hit them.

Planes rarely hammered at factories or army supply dumps. Such uses were limited by the size and abilities of the primitive sky machines themselves. But more limiting than anything was a lack of imagination on the part of the generals of the armies.

General Pershing had known the dangers of Moro swords, Indian arrows and Mexican rifles. But the brand-new horrors which the American Expeditionary Force of 1917-1918 had to face made swords, arrows, and rifles seem as primitive as clubs.

# 10
## Lafayette, We Are Here!

*"Wire me today whether you speak, read, and write French. . . ."*

One fine May morning John Joseph Pershing pondered these words as he stared at a telegram. He hesitated to answer. His fluency with the French language was—well, once he confessed it was "murder." The telegram from his father-in-law, Senator Warren, said that American troops soon would sail for France. Pershing knew that the Senator would try to see that J.J.P. would be one of their commanders.

Pershing sent the Senator an "optimistic" reply. J.J.P. said he used to speak French. Anyhow, he was sure he could relearn the language. (He never did, at least not very well.)

J.J.P. fibbed about his mastery of French, but the reason was that he was fiercely ambitious. He would have sacrificed a leg to be among the first to go overseas. However, five other generals outranked him. One of them surely would command the American forces. But at least Pershing hoped to be chosen for some lower job in the American Expeditionary Force, or the A.E.F., as it came to be called.

Colonel Theodore Roosevelt also ached to gallop into battle again. The old hero of San Juan Hill offered to serve as a sergeant—quite a demotion for a man who had been President of the United States! T.R. never went "Over There," but his four sons did.

Scholarly President Woodrow Wilson was studying some books that were new to him: War Department service records. He was impressed by what he read about one particular officer. Therefore Wilson asked that officer—John Joseph Pershing—to take command of the American Expeditionary Force. Once again Pershing was jumped over the heads of senior officers.

It was the crowning glory of his career. Yet Pershing was not altogether happy. Sadly he realized he would be a general without an army.

The United States had drafted no troops until the war engulfed her. Americans still had the innocent idea that a nation could "spring into arms overnight." Just as if they were living in the days of archers and pikemen.

Pershing's distress was brief. He lifted his chin. "There was no doubt in my mind of my ability to do my part," he wrote later. At the time, perhaps, his knees may have shaken a little.

J.J.P. chose a staff and began poring over the problems facing the baby A.E.F. For one thing, the number of training camps for the mobs of draftees could be counted on the fingers of one hand. There were only enough artillery shells in the whole country to last nine hours in battle. No machine guns whatever! (To the very end of the war, we bought and borrowed field guns and machine guns from the Allies.)

The raw draftees needed rifles. Some got the 1903 Springfields, fine bolt-action weapons. But J.J.P. had to buy more than two million Enfield rifles from England to help out.

Our air force had fifty-five rickety, unarmed planes. Pershing quickly threw fifty-one onto the junk pile. So our airmen flew British and French planes throughout most of our war in the clouds.

America's seagoing merchant fleet "had never recovered from the Civil War," according to Pershing. Therefore, more than half of the A.E.F. had to be moved and supplied by the battered ships of our Allies.

Our officer candidates were drilling with broomsticks. They heaved tomato cans as "pretend" hand grenades. So *this* was the brash nation that would wreck the war machine of the Kaiser? The British and French covered their smiles and made a polite suggestion. "Send us men," they offered, "and we will equip and teach them in our armies."

This was the one thing, first and last, that President Wilson and J.J.P. refused to grant. *The American Army would be American, and the American Army would fight its own battles.* Our A.E.F. never would be "a recruiting agency for either the French or the British," declared John Joseph Pershing. Defending this principle gave the General more white hairs than any menace he had to face.

Yet from the Allied point of view we were too late.

We would need too much time to train ourselves from scratch. The Eastern Front was becoming a splintered ruin. The Russians had been fighting both the Germans and Austrians in eastern Europe. Raw courage alone kept the Czar's men going. Often they charged, swinging empty rifles like clubs. Unarmed men followed close behind soldiers to pick up the rifles of those who fell. Some of the Russian front-line soldiers were women, too. The brave, bewildered Russians suffered nearly seven million dead and wounded during World War I, more than any other nation on either side.

Could America get into the fight before the Czar's armies crumbled? England and France trembled to think of a German victory on the Eastern Front. For then many thousands of the Kaiser's tough troops would be released for action against the Western Front defended by the British and the French.

Uncle Sam sent help on May 28, 1917. John Joseph Pershing and 190 men steamed for Europe on the liner *Baltic*. The tiny group was the core of the A.E.F.

When the *Baltic* docked, people jammed the pier at Liverpool, England, and shouted *huzza!* as the erect American general descended the gangplank. A guard of honor from the Royal Welsh Fusiliers clicked to present arms, bayonets flashing. Pershing smiled when he saw the Welshmen's mascot, a white billy goat. The Fusiliers were the regiment that had made the last dearly won charge up Breed's Hill (often miscalled Bunker Hill) back in 1775. Now their successors were saluting the first American soldier to land in England as an ally.

The British Crown showered honors on Pershing, not because he was Pershing but because he was the foremost symbol of America to the rescue. King George V entertained the former plowboy of Laclede. How soon could America ship over the 50,000 planes he had read about, asked King George. J.J.P. told the King not to believe everything he read in American newspapers. Then the two gentlemen went out to look at the Royal potatoes. Because of the food shortage the King's gardens were planted with vegetables instead of flowers that season.

Yes, England's welcome for J.J.P. was enthusiastic. But France's was positively wild. From Boulogne to Paris, mobs trailed the little band of Yanks yelling, *"Vive Persha-ing! Vive l'Amérique! Vive la France!"* Women were trampled underfoot trying to get close enough to kiss Pershing's hands or coat. But armed guards held the crowds back while bewhiskered generals kissed J.J.P. on both cheeks. Pershing had to get used to this old French custom.

In June "Pershing's Pets," the 1st Division, landed in France. The French government decided to celebrate the American Fourth of July. So a big parade with banners marched under the Arch of Triumph in Paris. The newly arrived Yanks strode along with it. Pershing bit his lips and thought his "pets" looked sloppy, but the Parisian girls loved them. Oo-la-la! These Americans were giants. Handsome, too! The doughboys grinned as they were pelted with flowers.

The happy ceremonies ended at the tomb of the Marquis de Lafayette. That young nobleman had helped our colonists during the gloom of the American Revolution. Now Americans were returning Lafayette's favor. Pershing almost missed the speeches at the cemetery. As usual he was a little late. But another American officer made a fine oration during which he bowed toward Lafayette's grave and said, "Lafayette, we are here!"

The phrase echoed across the ocean. Many Americans still think General Pershing coined it. But the man who did was another Midwesterner, Colonel C. E. Stanton, one of J.J.P.'s staff officers.

Pershing said he wished he had made "this striking

utterance" himself. However, J.J.P. never was much of
a fellow to strike sparks with words. One of his best
efforts came on July 8, 1917. It startled some people
and made others laugh.

He cabled Washington about how big the A.E.F.
must be. "A million men by May," the General wanted.
A million men by May? Why, there were only 14,000
in France! How under the blessed sun could the
United States ship 986,000 more in just ten months?

Many citizens here and abroad thought that Pershing had lost his mind. On July 11 they were *certain*
of it. "Plans for the future should be based on three
times this force," J.J.P. cabled, "that is, at least three
million men."

The kindest word our Navy had for Pershing's plan
was uttered by Admiral William D. Sims. Sims thought
the Army had a very dim sense of humor!

Three million men! An army twenty times the size
of Grant's blue coats of 1865! One hundred and fifty
times bigger than George Washington's biggest!

And Pershing expected this from a country whose
young officers had been drilling with broomsticks?

# 11
## Dumb John's Buttons

Newton D. Baker was a short man who wore rumpled suits and derby hats. His job was to run the War Department in President Wilson's cabinet. Some of Secretary Baker's political opponents grumbled that the War Department "needed a butcher, not a Baker." But little Mr. Baker faithfully upheld his President and his principal General.

Sometimes Pershing's neatness puzzled the slightly

untidy Secretary of War. "I cannot understand how a man with such vision and ability can be so interested in buttons," said Mr. Baker.

Young Americans drilling under the summer sun of 1917 agreed with Baker. But in very impolite words! Pershing had demanded that they learn discipline with a capital D. Buttons must be kept buttoned no matter how hot the day was. Shoes must be shined no matter how dusty the parade ground might be. And woe to the recruit whom the M.P.'s caught failing to salute an officer! "You're in the army now, you're not behind a plow!" was the accent of Pershing's discipline.

Even high-ranking officers were burned by J.J.P. if they fell down on their jobs. Once he summoned a red-faced major general into his office. The unhappy man stood sweating while the famous Pershing chin hardened. J.J.P.'s stare struck the general like a bayonet.

"And you call yourself a *soldier!*" Pershing barked. Then he proceeded to bawl out the general in "brimstone language."

No doughboy called Pershing "Papa" the way the *poilus* nicknamed their Marshal Joffre. Close friends seldom called him anything but "J.J.P." A lout of a touring Congressman shocked Europe by slapping

King Albert of Belgium upon his royal back. But nobody slapped the strict disciplinarian, J.J.P., on *his*
ramrod back.

Yet there was sense behind Pershing's severity. And
in the long run his iron-handedness was really kind.
He knew the military facts of life. Wars weren't Sunday School picnics. Easy-going officers could never
train themselves, let alone instruct raw rookies. And
dead soldiers could not rise for a second chance to
turn a defeat into a victory.

Few of J.J.P.'s generals had ever seen a unit even as
big as a regiment. Yet now—*whish!*—the draft was
tumbling recruits by the million into our training
camps. "Dumb Johns," the old soldiers called them.
These farmers, clerks, mill hands, students and hill-
billies were good material for an American Expeditionary Force, Pershing was sure. But they weren't
good *soldiers*, not yet.

"The German lines can, must and will be broken,"
he promised.

In Europe the Allied High Command gulped
sourly. What a nerve this American had! What did he
think they had been trying to do for three long years?
The French generals bemoaned their latest effort to
break the German lines. In April, 1917, they had lost

100,000 *poilus* fruitlessly. Afterwards some French regiments had mutinied, refusing to go over the top ever again. Their ringleaders were shot and the mutiny hushed up. Not a word leaked out to the English or American newspapers.

The British were pounding away at the Third Battle of Ypres when J.J.P. made his promise to break the enemy's lines. The battle ended with even greater loss than the French offensive. Over a quarter of a million Britons were killed, wounded or captured—a sacrifice that gained absolutely nothing.

No wonder this saucy American general dared to imply that the Allied "brass hats" did not know what they were doing!

Pershing suspected that he knew a flaw in the Allied scheme, one that was costing our friends dearly. In England J.J.P. had been shocked to hear that "nine weeks' training is long enough for trench warfare." In France he had noticed that the *poilus* had squatted in their trenches so long that they had forgotten basic soldiering. "Numerous instances were reported of men chasing an enemy throwing grenades at him instead of using a rifle." The *poilus* had forgotten how to shoot!

So Pershing demanded that the camps in the United States must hammer at rifle practice—and remember to keep buttons buttoned! He insisted that his officers must be attack-minded—and must be sure to enforce saluting.

Now what on earth was the connection between a doughboy's rifle and his buttons? What was the link between shooting and saluting?

The connection was plain to Pershing. Probably a soldier slouching around in a sloppy uniform also would carry a rusty rifle. And a doughboy who "didn't notice" when to salute an officer probably would be just as unaware of that officer when his whistle blew to signal an "over the top!" Strict discipline in small things was important because it made soldiers out of "Dumb Johns." And only trained, confident soldiers could win wars.

But, oh, how the young men in the dusty camps hated Pershing's "spit and polish!" They were footsore and homesick. Bugles commanded when to rise, when to eat, when to march, when to go to bed. Sergeants were a burden. And lieutenants—those ninety-day wonders! One artillery private glumly wrote that the only lieutenants he was going to like were the ones that got killed.

"Over There" was the war song that promised Europe "The Yanks are coming." The British were mocking it by adding, "When?" And Colonel Stanton's phrase, "Lafayette, we are here," was a sour joke among the French. They asked, "Where?"

Only 200,000 Yanks were "over there" by January, 1918, and these were half-trained and short of equipment. Many needed steel helmets to replace their felt campaign hats. Others lacked puttees. (These were spirally-wound woolen leggings we had adopted from the British.) The whole A.E.F. was poor in gas masks, trucks, machine guns and artillery. Camp buildings alone had cost us more than the Panama Canal, yet we were dragging far behind Pershing's timetable of "a million men by May."

As events turned out, the veteran German armies bogged down our schedule even worse.

The enemy's strategy was, "Hold the lines in the west and hit hard in the east." We have told how they held in the west. French troops had mutinied after their defeat; British manpower was bled white after the Third Battle of Ypres.

The Germans smashed at the Russians in the east. Revolution broke out against the Czar, and his armies melted away. *Bolsheviki* (Communists) seized control of the revolution, which was at first a democratic one. On December 23 the Communists signed an Armistice with the Kaiser. Russia was finished.

For good measure the Germans struck in the south too. In October, 1917, they smote the Italians at Caporetto in the Julian Alps. The surprised Italians fled, losing 300,000 men as prisoners alone. The rout continued down the mountains and across the north Italian plains, stopping just short of Venice. The Premier of Italy called for help. But the Allies were up to their eyes in their own gloomy problems.

Only on the high seas and in the Holy Land were there gleams of hope. The weary struggle against the U-boats was beginning to favor the Allies by the end of 1917. And in Palestine the Turks were fading. They hadn't liked their German partners much in the first place. A British army took Jerusalem in time to celebrate Christmas in the city sacred to three great world religions.

Still, the German High Command smiled as they exchanged a "Happy New Year" when 1918 began. With Russia beaten they had nothing to fear in the east. By spring the combined strength of all the German armies would crash against the Western Front. France would be overrun. The English would be chased across their Channel.

The Americans? *Ach,* the Yanks were not coming,

said the Germans. Not in time, anyhow. *Deutschland, Deutschland über alles!*—"Germany, Germany above all," they sang. *Der Tag*—The Day of victory was dawning with the new year!

## 12

## The Sergeant in the Hayloft

United States regular troops filed into the stinking
trenches of the Western Front on October 21, 1917.
Near by was the town of Lunéville. The Yanks pro-
nounced the name "Looneyville," of course. Lunéville
was not far from the province of Alsace, the original
home of the Pershing family. The commander of the
A.E.F. seemed destined to invade his ancestral home-
land. A group of French Alsatian exiles reminded

71

Pershing of this. They presented the General with a bouquet of flowers and pleaded to go "home" with him.

The forts around Lunéville were quiet. "Quiet sectors" were areas of the battlefront where the French and Germans caught their breath for big pushes elsewhere. Unarmed soldiers could wash their clothes, pick lice out of their shirts or kick a soccer ball around without having to dread the guns of their foes. The reason was that the foe was washing, picking and kicking, too. Sometimes *poilus* and Germans shared the same bathing holes.

The calm of Lunéville was shattered in the chilly dawn of November 3. The Germans had heard about the New World troops opposite them. They decided to treat the *Amerikaners* to a breakfast of shrapnel and high explosive. The German barrage landed on lines held by the 16th U.S. Infantry regiment. Company G was cut off. A swarm of booted Germans leaped over the top to raid the stunned company. When the enemy retired, they took along twelve prisoners and left three Yanks dead and five wounded. The first of 126,000 Americans to die during World War I were Privates Thomas F. Enright and Merle D. Hay and Corporal James B. Gresham.

More divisions landed in France. Each was two to four times bigger than the French, British or German units also called divisions. A trickle of half-trained doughboys was beginning to swell into a river of soldiers. And the river flowed toward Lorraine.

Lorraine—"with the accent on the rain," the Yanks swore. They mangled French words. Looneyville was one of the first. Later on the Ourcq River became the O'Rourke and Meurcy Ferme was Murphy's Farm and the Rhine River was the Ryan. The humor was heavy-footed but it pleased the Swedes, Greeks and Italians among the A.E.F., as much as the Irish.

All the boys agreed about the accent on the *rain* in Lorraine. The winter of 1917-18 had been the worst of the war, and the seasons that followed were soakers. The Yanks would have to slog through mud, push cannon through mud and fight in mud. Wounded men would drown in shell holes because they could not clamber up the slippery sides of the craters.

Why did General Pershing choose this particular part of "sunny France" to fight in? You can be sure he didn't feel sentimental about the Alsatians and their bouquet of posies. There had to be firmer reasons, and there were.

The five-hundred-mile siege of the trench war zigzagged from Belgium in the northwest to neutral Switzerland in the southeast. The Belgians naturally wanted to fight the invaders of their country near home. So they manned the upper end of the line. Next came the British. They had to protect the Channel seaports which were their links to England. The French controlled the rest of the line down to the Alps. The *poilus* watched especially the sector between the Aisne River and Verdun. This vital zone shielded Paris, their capital. Gray-clad Germans and blue-clad Frenchmen trampled their comrades' dead bodies in battle after battle at Verdun. *One million men died or were wounded at this one place alone.* But "They shall not pass" was the slogan of the heroic *poilus* of Verdun. And the Germans never did pass.

The weary French needed our relief most. West of Verdun was the Argonne Forest; eastward were the rough, tough Vosges Mountains. This sector became J.J.P.'s choice for America's battleground.

Pershing did not pick his ground merely to please the French. Again, there had to be a firmer reason, and there was. The General's keen eye saw that his A.E.F. could not use the same supply routes already overloaded by his Allies. He had to explore new ones. Therefore Pershing selected little-used Atlantic ports like St. Nazaire, La Pallice and Bassens to land his troops. From these towns the A.E.F., with bag and baggage, was shunted across southern France. Their battleground was as far from salt water ports as Cleveland is, or Memphis or Tucson.

Moving the doughboys was a titanic job. Docks and piers had to be built. Railroads were patched up or laid new. Ships had to be found to float the troops; locomotives had to be assembled to haul them. Time was running against us. The Allies looked weak and the Germans strong. Pershing was certain that if we did not make our weight felt by 1919 at the latest— well, then, good-by France.

The U-boats had sent thousands of ships down to Davy Jones's locker. A shortage of shipping plagued Pershing to the end of the war. And years of abuse had crippled the French railroads. The doughboys were amused by the unusual look of the little French trains. One said their engines sounded as if they were giggling. The four-wheeled freight cars were marked "40 Hommes/8 Cheveaux," meaning that they could handle either forty men *or* eight horses. The Yanks pretended this was funny—there wasn't anything for them to do but laugh about Forty-and-Eight.

Somehow the big moving job was done. The war

was won sooner than J.J.P. had dared to guess. A single example shows how well the A.E.F.'s Service of Supply, under General James G. Harbord, finally worked. At eight o'clock one morning late in 1918 the big depot at Gievres got a "chow" order from the front. The hungry doughboys wanted:

> 1,125,000 cans of tomatoes
> 1,000,000 pounds of sugar
> 600,000 cans of corned beef or "corned willie"
> 750,000 pounds of a hash often called "monkey meat"
> 150,000 pounds of beans which had various nicknames.

The supply depot had all this food. And the sweating Quartermaster loaded and shipped it off *by six o'clock* the *same day.*

The final reason General Pershing determined to attack on the Lorraine front also was a matter of transportation—*German* transportation. Right behind the enemy's lines was the mighty fortress of Metz. Metz was to the Germans what Verdun was for the French. If the Yanks cracked the last trench system (the so-called Hindenburg Line) in Lorraine, they could seize Metz. The city, capital of the old province, was the hinge of the whole enemy position. Two railroads that stitched the German armies together crossed here. And many of the finest steel mills and coal mines of Germany were protected by the fortress city.

J.J.P. knew that the Germans would fight like wolves to hold Metz. American dead might stack up like another Verdun. This horror must not be, vowed the General.

So he slaved to prevent it. Pershing's usual day began at seven in the morning and ended at midnight. He drove here, there, everywhere—a grim and tireless man. He was a terror, J.J.P. was. He snapped at generals and privates alike for sloppy behavior. He ordered court-martial punishments, pestered the War Department in Washington, and dipped into the cook pots to taste the doughboys' "slum" for himself. But the General never failed to visit hospitals during his lightning tours of inspection. The care of the sick and the wounded was important to him, too.

"Your men must feel that you are doing the very best you can for them," he told his young officers.

Pershing even crawled up ladders in stables to see

77

how his men were bedded down. So did the Frenchman, General Philippe Pétain. Pétain commanded the
*poilus* after their mutiny in 1917. One day the two
gentlemen met in a shadowy hayloft. Pétain mistook
Pershing for the sergeant in charge of the Yank pla-
toon quartered there. He asked friendly questions:

How did the sergeant get along with the *poilus?*

Did the sergeant get an egg to eat every now and
then?

Would the sergeant like to visit France in peacetime?

The "sergeant" stood at respectful attention and
answered the Frenchman's questions. "I played the
part of a sergeant the best I could," Pershing explained
afterwards.

Later Pétain was told by hilarious members of his
own staff who the "sergeant in the hayloft" really was.

You never could tell about John Joseph Pershing. An
Englishman said J.J.P. was "a man silent in seventeen
languages." His own superior, Secretary of War Baker,
never understood the General's passion for neat buttons. Nobody ever praised Pershing for his sense of
humor.

And yet John Joseph Pershing once "played the part
of a sergeant" the best he could. Possibly he was

having mild fun at Pétain's expense. More likely he was trying to save the kindly Frenchman from embarrassment. Anyhow, the result was a strong and lasting friendship between the two men.

# 13

## Tough Kitty of Cantigny

"Tommy Atkins" is a name given to any soldier of
England. Mr. Rudyard Kipling wrote a poem about
him although the poet did not invent the old nickname. The Tommies of 1917 called the first American
troops they saw "Sammies." Tommy reasoned, "W'y
not? Ain't the blokes sons of Uncle Sam?"

These "Sammies" (the nickname never caught on)
were Corps of Engineers regulars. They worked in

northern France with the British army. An engineer-soldier must be able to switch from his hammer and saw to a rifle and bayonet at the drop of a shell. Our engineers had to use *all* their tools at Cambrai in November of 1917. Theirs were among the very first American shots of World War I.

The engineers pitched into the fight again the following spring. They stood with Tommy Atkins to stop a German thrust along the river Somme in March, 1918. The enemy was beginning a series of far-flung attacks that would last until midsummer.

At first things went very badly for our friends. The Germans had carefully plotted their assaults under code names like "Mars," "Achilles" and so on. General Erich von Ludendorff's forces outnumbered the Allies, too. His Eastern Front armies had joined him after the knockout of Russia. The German strategist decided first to sweep the Tommies out of France.

German guns roared against the Tommies along a front one hundred miles long. Thousands of poison gas shells burst among the explosives. Deep-dug trenches were wiped out with all the men in them. Many Tommies were buried alive by the blasts. German planes swept the skies. Even the weather hurt the Tommies for the battlefields were smothered by fog.

German bayonets jabbed forward under cover of a natural smoke screen.

The Tommies reeled back under the attack. They counted 300,000 casualties and 975 cannon lost in two months.

When the British were staggering, the Germans hit the French too. Soon the whole Allied line was wavering, and a shudder of panic shook Europe. General Pershing's prophecy that the war would not be won in the trenches was being proved right. The horror was that the enemy was proving it. Ludendorff had been practicing his men in open-field tactics all winter. The Germans were not burrowing like gophers any more— they were stampeding like crazy cattle.

At the height of the peril, J.J.P. drove out to talk to General Foch. Pershing's blue eyes were troubled, but they enjoyed the sight of handsome poplar trees along the hilly road. His mind brooded over problems that seemed to be mocked by the fine spring day. Not far from his headquarters he ordered his chauffeur to stop his big staff-car. Pershing delivered food to a French family he had met. Their little daughter always got a special piece of cake or candy for herself from the hard-boiled General.

Pershing needed occasional peaceful pauses like

this. He had been having a vexing time. The A.E.F. fumbled along for lack of ships. Supplies piled up on the wharves at home but did Pershing no good abroad. Even in France J.J.P. was having trouble with transportation. The local farmers refused to sell him horses. The peasants hoped the rich Americans would send over their own horses. Then after the war what a bargain sale there would be of American army surplus animals! All farmers love sales, and the French farmer is no exception.

General Foch was giving J.J.P. a bad time too. The Frenchman never seemed to want to help the A.E.F. to ship over their own heavy artillery, trucks and so forth. All he wanted were Yanks to fill up the thinned ranks of his French armies. So did Lord Douglas Haig, the British commander. Pershing monotonously repeated no, no, no. *Americans would fight as an American army, and that was that!*

The heads of the Allied governments also wheedled, badgered and threatened Pershing. Premier David Lloyd George of Britain, Georges Clemenceau of France, and Vittorio Orlando of Italy all took turns hammering at the General. But the one-time farm boy of Laclede told the statesmen, "No, I have made up my mind." And he walked out of their presence, head held high, secure in the knowledge that his own President supported him. The premiers of the Allied countries agreed sadly that this Pershing was a very bullheaded fellow.

The German successes partly changed J.J.P.'s mind. If the Allies cracked wide open, there never would be an American Army. So he had to back down on his principle of not allowing his men to be used to replace Tommies and *poilus*—for the time being. The big divisions of generals Bullard, Bundy and Dickman might be broken up—for the time being. The Lorraine campaign would have to be postponed—for the time being.

Outside of Foch's headquarters on a certain spring day, J.J.P. paused to view the fresh flowers and new grass. He bent down a bough of cherry blossoms to smell them. Then he squared his broad shoulders and marched into the castle.

Courteously he saluted General Foch. "I have come to tell you that the American people would consider it a great honor for our troops to be engaged in the present battle," Pershing said. "All that we have are yours. Use them as you wish."

Foch fervently kissed J.J.P. on both cheeks!

"Use them as you wish" was sincere, but J.J.P.

meant it only for the duration of the emergency.

The best-trained of the seven American divisions at the booming front were the 1st, 2nd, and 3rd, regulars all. Secret code called them "Kitty," "Jennie" and "Minnie" at that time, according to Pershing's biographer, Frederick Palmer.

The 1st Division faced the German-held town of Cantigny in Picardy. Here the enemy had stabbed his deepest into the French lines. General Foch asked Pershing to try to take Cantigny. Kitty, the 1st Division, was selected, and the young staff officer who planned the first American attack of World War I was Colonel George C. Marshall. Twenty-three years later Marshall directed our global war against both Hitler and the Japanese. Later still he organized the Marshall Plan to put Europe on its feet after Hitler had wrecked it.

The 28th Infantry Regiment of the 1st Division carried the Stars and Stripes in the assault. The doughboys were backed up by French tanks, guns and flame throwers. The helpful French also were curious; they sent along photographers to record how the untested Yanks would behave.

On May 28, 1918, the 28th went over the top along a mile-long front. Overhead buzzed friendly shells

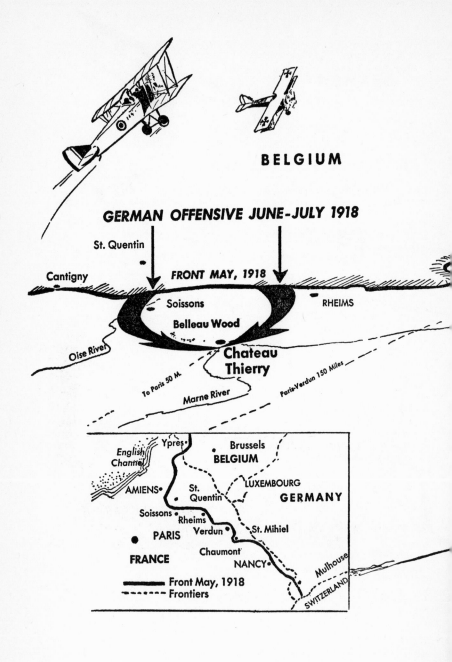

BELGIUM

**GERMAN OFFENSIVE JUNE-JULY 1918**

St. Quentin

Cantigny

**FRONT MAY, 1918**

Soissons

Belleau Wood

RHEIMS

Oise River

Chateau Thierry

To Paris 50 M.

Marne River

Paris-Verdun 150 Miles

Ypres·

Brussels

English Channel

**BELGIUM**

AMIENS·

St. Quentin

LUXEMBOURG

**GERMANY**

Soissons ·

Rheims

**PARIS**

Verdun

St. Mihiel

**FRANCE**

Chaumont

NANCY

Mulhouse

SWITZERLAND

▬▬▬▬ Front May, 1918
--------- Frontiers

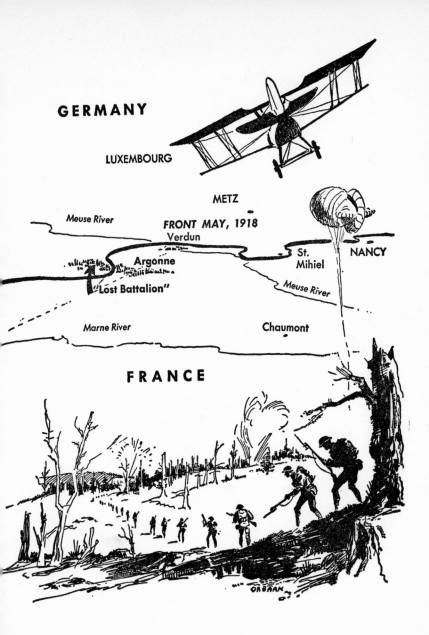

GERMANY

LUXEMBOURG

METZ

Meuse River

FRONT MAY, 1918
Verdun

St.
Mihiel

NANCY

Argonne

Meuse River

"Lost Battalion"

Marne River

Chaumont

FRANCE

ORBAAN

that threw up slowly creeping fountains of explosions nearer and nearer to Cantigny. Behind the rolling barrage, the Yanks plodded heavily up a hill toward the town. Not all of the boys who stumbled going up the grade ever got to their feet again. Not all who fell were merely tripped by rusted barbed wire. The Germans had big guns too. And in the village Maxim machine guns chattered at the Yanks from cellar windows. Sharpshooters and "pineapple" grenades finally put the Maxims out of business.

Cantigny was won. Yet the "dashing little victory" of Kitty captured few headlines. The reason was that the Germans stole the show elsewhere on a much bigger stage.

The day before the fight at Cantigny the enemy had unleashed a furious drive along the Chemin des Dames. That means "the Ladies' Road," but it was no place for a lady between May 27 and June 3, 1918. The region wasn't a happy place even for the battle-wise French *poilus*.

General Pétain had to recall the guns he had loaned the Yanks to bombard Cantigny. So by a wretched twist of fate American deaths in Cantigny were greater *after* winning the ruined town than during our attack. Kitty's doughboys had to suffer a pound-

General Pershing fords the Rio Grande chasing Pancho Villa.

Wooden guns and half-uniforms served the Yanks in 1917.

"Billboards splashed army and navy recruiting posters far and wide."

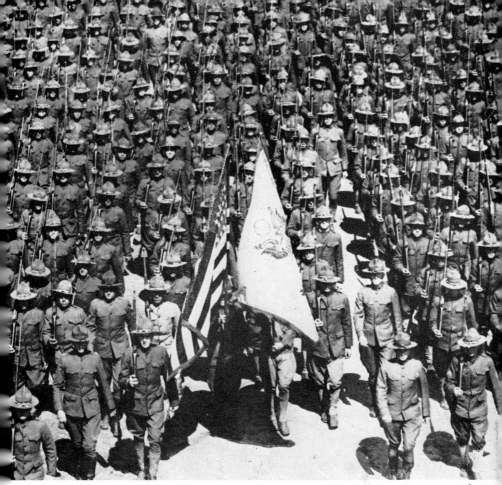

"And we won't come back 'til it's over, over there."

"The machine gun was king of the battlefield." These Germans were firing on the American 28th Division, at Chateau-Thierry, July, 1918.

"Purely an engine of death." A German U-boat surrenders on the high seas.

"Every inch the soldier"—Pershing lands at Cherbourg, France.

An early British tank, like "Mother," described in Chapter 9.

Germans crouch to go "over the top."

No Man's Land, where "trees were stripped sticks in a wilderness of ruin."

*Right top:* The British go "over the top."

*Right bottom:* Marshal Foch and General John J. Pershing.

*Bettmann Archive*

*Wide World Photos*

Aerial dogfights were "a graceful, murderous ballet."

Captain Eddie Rickenbacker, "a cool pilot."

"Lafayette, here we go!" Yanks marching under the Arch of Triumph, Paris, 1918.

Victory parade in New York City, 1918.

ing by German artillery without replying. Yet they hugged the good earth and mowed down waves of infantry counterattackers by accurate rifle fire. Cantigny remained the property of tough Kitty.

However, the Chemin des Dames area became German. Ludendorff's shock troops smashed ahead forty miles and swept up 65,000 prisoners along with tons of military loot. No Allied planes had been watching the crafty foe. In total secrecy the Germans had massed an army and flung it against a quiet sector. German hobnailed boots clumped on to the river Marne in a mere four days—closer to Paris than they had been since the taxicab-army fight in 1914. The French capital itself felt enemy gunfire. A giant railroad cannon heaved shells into Paris from as far as seventy-five miles away. No gun in history ever has shot so far.

Panic gripped the Parisians. Frightened people fled from their city by auto, by horse and by shoe leather. General Pershing heard that one million citizens poured out of Paris that spring.

The gentlemen of the Allied Supreme War Council gathered at the Palace of Versailles just outside Paris. They could feel the thudding of heavy German howitzers through the soles of their feet from the palace floor. The shaking earth also made the crystal chandeliers tinkle over the heads of the sober men. Generals Foch and Pétain and England's Field Marshal Lord Haig sat and talked and worriedly chewed their mustaches. (Oddly enough, all the top generals of every army wore mustaches during World War I.)

Georges Clemenceau, the bald old Premier of France, was there too. His mustache was a droopy, soup-strainer type, easy to chew. But the Tiger of France, as he was called, snarled instead. "I will fight in front of Paris. I will fight in Paris. I will fight behind Paris," roared the old Tiger, even as the palace shook around him from the battle raging so close by.

Pershing's mustache was not bushy enough to chew conveniently, but he was as worried as the rest. He could have said "I told you so" to his allies at the palace table. J.J.P.'s intelligence section had predicted a German drive along the Chemin des Dames. Their prophecy was ignored. What experienced Frenchman could have believed that green Yank officers might be wise?

Philippe Pétain called on Pershing for instant help. The American acted at once. Kitty, his 1st Division, already was engaged. Now came the turn of her sisters, Jennie and Minnie, the 2nd and 3rd Divisions.

# 14
## Jennie and Minnie Go to a Party

"Crank 'er up, buddy!"

"Where are we going to?"

"Crank 'er up and we'll find out!"

Two machine gunners of the 7th Battalion, 3rd Division, could have exchanged these words on the morning of May 30, 1918. The gunners had been training near Pershing's headquarters at Chaumont. They were getting to be good gunners, but they were getting bored too. Now suddenly came marching orders from the boss, Pershing himself! The excited gunners buckled on their tin hats, piled their weapons into motor trucks and rattled off.

The fighting at the Marne River was only 110 miles away, but the 7th Battalion needed twenty-two hours to get there. Tires blew out, engines died and axles broke. Night driving without lights caused collisions. The wheezy trucks often needed to be pushed up hills or out of mud holes. The disgusted gunners who shoved behind a wheel spinning in mud must have wished for their beloved Army mules.

Even when the trucks were jolting along under their own power, they ran into human delays. Groups of haggard old Frenchmen, or women with babies, stumbled into the advancing American column. But despite refugees, mud and breakdowns, the machine gunners reached the Marne a full day ahead of their foot-slogging infantry buddies. Even at a five-mile-an-hour pace the trucks were faster than "shoe-leather express." The entire 3rd Division lined up beside the French east of Château-Thierry by nightfall of June 1.

Château-Thierry lay in France's bread basket. The fields of ripening wheat about the town were broken

by patches of well-kept woods. Across the narrow
Marne River was the enemy. The swirling battle was
so tangled, however, that some Germans were on the
French bank of the river and some *poilus* were on the
enemy's side.

Campaigns bewilder the individual men fighting
in them. Suppose you had been a doughboy with the
2nd Division that June. You would have packed to
march north on foot to relieve your own 1st Division
at Cantigny. But, next thing you knew, you were rum-
bling eastward in a truck to help the French at the
Marne. If you survived the war, you could buy a book
when you got home to find out what the good old 2nd
—and you—had done!

The regulars of the 2nd ran into streams of refugees too, just as the 3rd had. Their trucks had to creep
slowly to avoid farm carts piled high with children,
chickens, clocks and mattresses. Among the sorry tide
were many wild-eyed *poilus*. "You are too late!" they
shouted to the Yanks. "Flee! All is lost!"

However, the great bulk of the stubborn French
army was holding on when the 2nd reached the
Marne. The doughboys dug in across the main high-
way leading to Paris. Their own 3rd Division linked

on to the 2nd's left flank. Several badly mauled French divisions were able to pull back for regrouping. They left Jennie and Minnie, the 2nd and 3rd Divisions, to stand fast against the victory-mad enemy.

"It must have been a relief when the worn and tired French soldiers caught sight of Americans hurrying forward to battle," said J.J.P.

The Yanks stopped the Germans dead. And within a week Jennie and Minnie were counterattacking. No large body of the enemy except prisoners ever crossed the Marne at Château-Thierry.

Pershing was mightily pleased and proud. He hastened to General Foch. Now was the moment to strike hard, he urged. If the French were breathless, wouldn't the Germans be getting pretty exhausted, too?

For the time being Foch was too glum to discuss the matter. But Monsieur André Tardieu was only too willing to talk. M. Tardieu was an official of the French government and also was something of a busybody. He declared that in his opinion the officer staff of the A.E.F. was weak.

M. Tardieu was entitled to his opinion. But he chose a bad time to deliver it to the elated Pershing. J.J.P.'s manner changed abruptly. His blue eyes turned to an angry gray, and his fighting chin shot out.

"If you people will cease troubling yourselves so much about our affairs and attend strictly to your own," his voice crackled, "we'll all get along much better!" He had listened to enough "of that sort of nonsense!"

Meanwhile, the 2nd Division was writing a page of history in blood. Half the division were marines, and half was regular infantry. The Germans were shooting down their throats from the high ground between Belleau Wood and the town of Vaux. So the Marine Brigade banged through the bushes of Belleau Wood, while the Infantry Brigade stormed through the wheat toward Vaux. They "rushed into the fight as though to a party," exclaimed the admiring French general Mangin.

By July 9, the 2nd had cleared the high ground and wiped out the enemy in Belleau Wood and Vaux. Poison gas clung to the shrubbery of the woods, choking and burning the marines. Shrapnel and TNT ripped the doughboys in the exposed wheat fields. They won, but back in the States many blue stars in service flags hanging in windows were changed to gold stars. The golden ones meant that some boys never would return to Portland or Birmingham or Detroit. To win a miserable mile of forest and field, the gallant 2nd Division lost one man out of almost every four who "rushed into the . . . party."

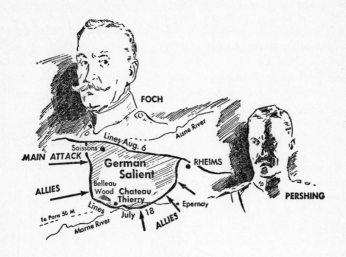

# 15
# The Turn of the Tide

Historians tell us that America's doughboys added "a stiffening of cement" to the Allied lines at the Marne. Yet the fights at Château-Thierry, Belleau Wood and Vaux were only defensive victories. But General Ferdinand Foch's heart was lifted by them.

Foch was a Basque, one of a race of hardy mountaineers from the Pyrennees Mountains. He was clever, tough and virile. He determined to widen the counter-

97

offensive begun by the Americans along the blood-stained Marne. With J.J.P. and Pétain, Foch bent over a map to plan their blows.

They saw an ugly bulge in the Allied line. This salient, as bulges are called by military men, was thirty-five miles wide and twenty deep. The town of Château-Thierry formed the point of the salient; the river Aisne bounded the northern base of the rough triangle. Many Germans were dug into the area, and more were coming. They were led by the Crown Prince of Germany in person.

Poor Crown Prince Friedrich Wilhelm Viktor August Ernst von Hohenzollern! He wasn't a very good general, and he never inherited the crown of Germany. Friedrich Wilhelm had a neck as long as his name, but practically no chin. He was lanky and stooped and wore a monocle and a waxed mustache. Newspaper cartoonists used to label him "the Clown Prince"!

General Foch selected four French armies, including American units, to lead in his Aisne-Marne punch. J.J.P.'s contribution to Foch's knockout blow was seven divisions. The regular 1st, 2nd, 3rd and 4th were already in the lines. Joining them were the 26th New England National Guard, the 28th Pennsylvania National Guard, and the all-American 42nd, the Rainbow Division. Behind the front waited nineteen more of the double-sized American divisions.

On July 4, 1918, the A.E.F. was just under the "million men by May" that Pershing had asked for. "What a difference it would have made if the Allies had given us ships earlier!" J.J.P. sighed. Yet now he was preparing to land *four* million men by *next* May!

The A.E.F. was short on training and heavy equipment, but their "enthusiasm more than offset their lack of experience," Pershing was sure. He felt deeply honored when Foch chose three American divisions to be "the point of the lance" to be hurled at the Crown Prince.

Like most battles in modern times the Aisne-Marne drive really was a series of battles. French howitzers and 75s opened the ball with a clangor of drumfire at 4.35 A.M. on July 18. (The 75-mm. field gun was a famous cannon. It was not automatic. But some Yank gunners amused themselves by trying to fire it as fast as a pistol, and succeeded in banging off forty shells a minute.) There was no lull in the shelling, gassing, marching, screaming, bombing and killing until the middle of September. French and Americans fought until they collapsed. Fresh men replaced them, and the battle raged on without letup.

Yet the crucial period was the first three days, as the Chancellor of Germany confessed. After July 21, Herr von Hertling groaned, "Even the most optimistic among us understood that all was lost. The history of the world was played out in three days."

The Germans scarcely knew what hit them. The Crown Prince was shocked. He had been whipping the French ahead of him, only to have the fierce *poilus* about-face and whip *him!* The German commander in chief, Erich von Ludendorff, had piled mountains of supplies into the Crown Prince's salient. The bulge was a swelling sack full of men ready to burst out toward Paris. Then suddenly the Crown Prince found himself in a bag, with "beaten" enemies pulling the neck of the sack shut.

What caused the turn of the tide, as writers have called the Aisne-Marne?

First, the grogginess of the Germans. A nation of sixty million people, no matter how efficient and valiant they might be, can't whip the world. Yet Germany had been trying for four bloody years with little outside help. As J.J.P. had suspected, the Imperial German Army was tired. Victories can be as exhausting as defeats. By the end of the summer of 1918, our Yanks were taking some pitiable prisoners. There were white-bearded grandpas in the Kaiser's army then. Other soldiers were too small to fill out their gray-green uniforms—it is said that some were only twelve years old.

Nevertheless the Germans were not routed at the Aisne-Marne, nor anywhere else. The Crown Prince withdrew slowly, taking away most of his precious supplies.

Another reason the tide turned was the skill of Ferdinand Foch. As a military chess player the Frenchman was more canny than Erich von Ludendorff.

But the main reason Foch won was that he had more men. Nearly 300,000 fresh doughboys joined his big push at the Marne. Their numbers, added to the *poilus*, swamped the Germans. One out of six Yanks was killed or wounded. But after July 21, the star of the Kaiser began to sink into darkness.

Because World War II with Hitler was so much bigger than World War I, some people think the A.E.F. played a mere game with the Germans. Not so! Behold the case of the 28th Division. The Pennsylvanians went in at Château-Thierry and fought almost without letup for five months. Pershing dubbed them his Iron Division because of their dogged stand at St.

Agnan, where "they slew the flower of the Kaiser's Army and piled them up like cordwood." The Germans themselves called the 28th "The Bloody Buckets" because of the red keystone shoulder patch of the Pennsylvanians. But the blood in the bucket wasn't all German. The 28th lost 14,000 men before the armistice.

Château-Thierry had been a pretty little country town. When the battle passed on, the place was a smoking ruin. "Nothing remained but latitude, longitude, and broken brick," said an awed American gunner who had helped to demolish Château-Thierry. But the smash of the Allies was so swift that French peasants were able to move back in time to harvest their wheat. This also was a disappointment for the Germans. They had counted on that grain themselves for their slowly starving people at home.

Was Pershing nervous during the campaign? Was he fidgety, did he fret?

Not our plowboy from Laclede. "I never worry," said John Joseph Pershing. "When the day's work is over, I go to sleep."

Nevertheless strain was showing on him. His hair was turning white. The tough General relaxed when he could by taking horseback rides and by attending children's parties.

A school near his headquarters held graduation exercises on July 14. This is France's Bastille Day, comparable to our Fourth of July. It was a quiet Sunday at Chaumont that day in 1918. Only the bees buzzed in the clover, and the children giggled on the lawn. Pershing knew that in just four days he would have to throw thousands of his fellow Americans into the furnace of battle. Yet the handsome General laughed and joked with the little French children as he gave out prizes. He didn't seem to have a care in the world.

When they gave him a present, J.J.P. wrote about it in his diary, just as though he had received a decoration from President Poincaré of the Republic of France. The children's gift was a book, *Episodes from the History of France*. They hoped little nine-year-old Warren, Pershing's son, would enjoy it.

"We shall long treasure it," the General promised.

# 16

## German Meets "German"

J.J.P. once pointed to the big map on the wall of his headquarters. Colored pins and tapes marked the battle lines of the various fronts.

"Look what the German army has done to the Allies," he said. "It has blown a balloon into their lines."

The General mused awhile. Then he murmured, "The Germans have a great army. I have German blood in my veins, too. But we will give them as good as they send, German against German, and better!"

In the Grimpettes Woods, the Kaiser's Germans bumped up against some of J.J.P.'s "Germans." This combat was just one of the many forming the Aisne-Marne campaign. The American division engaged was the 32nd, from Wisconsin and Michigan. Many of the boys bore names like Straussmeyer, Kraut and so on. Many spoke fluent German because German was used around their homes—the homes of Mid-western loggers, brewers, cheese-makers and farmers. One company of the 32nd included members of a *mannerchor* (men's choir) who utterly baffled a group of German prisoners.

The dejected German prisoners were being herded toward our rear when they heard singing. It was a beautiful, full-throated male chorus. Tenors, baritones and basses all knew their parts perfectly. As the singers approached the crown of a hill, concealed from the prisoners, the Germans suddenly realized what song they were hearing: the old German national anthem, *Die Wacht Am Rhein!*

The Germans shot furtive looks at their guards. The stirring "Watch on the Rhine"! Did it mean that their comrades had captured the American rear? But the guards showed no concern—how strange! Then the unmistakable flat helmets of an American column began to bob and rise over the hill. One of the prisoners snatched at a last wild hope: maybe the *mannerchor* singers were the Kaiser's men in disguise.

"Where do you come from?" he asked one of the passing singers.

"Milwaukee, bud," said the Yank briefly.

The enemy who attacked the Grimpettes Woods must have been equally dumbfounded. The Yanks yelled at the enemy in good German. The fighting raged in pitch darkness. Bayonet clashed against bayonet in the underbrush. Nobody asked mercy. It was a duel to the death accompanied by grunts, groans and sudden shrill screams. When dawn broke, the only German Germans left in the woods were lying still. The German-American 32nd Division had "given better than they got."

Unhappily, back in the United States, if you had a German accent some people hated you automatically. Our super-patriots even tried to change the name of sauerkraut to "Liberty cabbage." Store windows bearing German names were smashed by hoodlums. In the eyes of the hoodlums, it was even unpatriotic to own a dachshund because the Kaiser liked those dogs. Public schools dropped their German language classes, and the state of Nebraska passed a law making a father a criminal if he should teach his own children the tongue. Such dreadful nonsense did not happen everywhere, but it did happen.

Wartime is a time of distrust, always. Yet in some ways we were able to gain because America is a melting pot of many lands and races.

Three Yanks captured a German army cook because they all could talk the Slovak tongue. The prisoner began to cook for his captors with great appreciation on both sides. Naturally, this was strictly against Army regulations, but who cared?

A Signal Corps soldier was ordered to install a field telephone in a big dugout selected for an American headquarters. (Dugouts were underground rooms opening off the trenches.) The Yank popped into the dugout right in the arms of nine Germans. "He told them he wanted to put in a phone. They objected and he insisted," was the way the army newspaper, *The Stars and Stripes*, reported it. A fight started. The Yank broke the telephone over the skull of an enemy, who cried out in Polish. The fight ended. All nine Germans surrendered to the Signal Corps man, who was a native of Poland. So were five of the Germans.

Wires were tapped by both sides whenever pos-

sible. The German monitors who listened to our con-
versations had been trained to understand dozens of
languages. But one American headquarters "foxed"
all the enemy linguists. Its orders were transmitted over
the wires by Navajo Indian message-senders and re-
ceivers. Very few people speak Navajo except the
Navajos. No German could.

John Joseph Pershing could not follow rapid French
well. He used an interpreter to be sure he knew pre-
cisely what his French allies were saying. However,
even if J.J.P. had been able to speak French like a Parisian he still would have had difficulty making his points
with Marshal Foch.

The Frenchman had been promoted to Marshal in
August, 1918, in recognition of his victory over the
Germans at the Marne. He still was Commander in
Chief of the Allied armies. Foch could not force the
British or Americans to accept his ideas. But they
agreed to allow him to guide the overall strategy of
the war.

Now that the enemy had been halted, J.J.P. was
assembling his independent American army. Foch
had pledged support of this plan after many bitter
arguments. The First Army, A.E.F., gathered in Lor-

raine for an attack on St. Mihiel. But at the last moment Foch changed his mind!

"There is no time to do such a thing," said the Marshal.

Pershing's temper boiled, but he suppressed it. He protested that very elaborate preparations would be wasted. The sector for American operations had been chosen for a long time. Pershing reminded Foch that the independent American army had been postponed only because of the crisis at Château-Thierry.

Foch refused to budge. He insulted J.J.P. by suggesting that the new First American Army become a French one under a French commander.

Pershing rose to his feet, "his jaw hard set," according to one witness.

"Marshal Foch, you have no authority to call upon me to yield my command of the American army," J.J.P. said. "You cannot scatter it among the Allied forces where it will not be an American army at all."

The Frenchman got up to face Pershing. Foch was not so tall as Pershing, but he was broad and bulky.

"I must insist upon the arrangement," the Marshal snapped. He hinted that he would take up Pershing's behavior with President Wilson directly.

For the space of a heartbeat the two officers glared at each other in silence. Later Pershing admitted that he felt a strong urge to punch the stubborn Frenchman. But he fought for self-control and won. If Pershing had struck Foch, President Wilson would have been convinced that J.J.P. should be replaced by an American general who knew how to keep his temper.

Swiftly J.J.P. strode out of the room.

His friend and admirer, General Pétain, smoothly arranged another meeting between the disputants. That time the three generals talked calmly, and a compromise resulted. Pershing was to go ahead with a limited attack on St. Mihiel. Also he received assurances there would be no more heckling about putting the First Army under a foreign commander. Foch in turn took J.J.P.'s word that he would shift the A.E.F. to the Meuse-Argonne line by September 25.

How on earth could he do it, Pershing wondered. It was a task for *two* American armies.

But do it he did. There is a cocky military saying that fits Pershing and his A.E.F: "The difficult thing we do at once; the impossible takes a little longer!"

# 17
## St. Mihiel

General Pershing decided to command America's first
big-scale offensive personally. He created a First
Army of the American Expeditionary Force on August 10, 1918. Under J.J.P. worked the First Army's
corps generals: Hunter Liggett, Joseph T. Dickman
and George H. Cameron. They had just thirty days
to get ready.

Motorcycle couriers bounced over the cobblestoned

streets of Neufchateau to speed orders from First Army Headquarters to the Army's 550,000 doughboys. High-ranking officers bustled about asking questions, making suggestions and getting their assignments. Pershing was the center of the frenzy of activity. Yet when his battle plan was printed, it covered only four-teen pages. The old French general whom J.J.P. re-lieved at St. Mihiel courteously had turned over his own plan of attack to the American—all 300 pages of it!

As the day of battle drew nearer, Pershing moved up closer to the trenches at a place called Ligny-en-Barrois. Here he had his hot argument with Marshal Foch. The Frenchman wished to cancel such vast works as these:

The 295 miles of railroad laid by American en-gineers and leading into the St. Mihiel sector.

The 40,000 tons of ammunition Ordnance and Quartermaster troops had dumped behind the Amer-icans' jump-off line.

The huge radio and telephone network the Signal Corps had woven. Carrier pigeons also waited to take off whenever wires broke.

The sixty-five hospital trains and 20,900 beds moved into the area by the Medical Corps.

Pershing's rage at Marshal Foch was more than the fury of wounded pride. He simply could not tolerate the waste of his A.E.F.'s hard work.

Yet when Foch finally approved a limited assault on St. Mihiel, the Marshal generously helped his New World allies. The 3,000 cannon the Yanks used came from Foch, and French gunners manned half of them. All the 267 light tanks were French, and a third were driven by Frenchmen. Foch also ordered 100,000 *poilus* to support the doughboys. Britain and France both loaned us pilots and planes. Colonel Billy Mitchell's air armada of 1400 planes was the largest the world had known up to that day.

The generous help we received from our Allies was vital to our men. America did not win the war singlehanded, as some people boasted afterward. Our doughboys tipped the scales toward victory—with the aid of heavy contributions from England and France.

The Battle of St. Mihiel exploded in the night of September 12, 1918. A four-hour bombardment of the first-line German trenches heaved tons of mud and dirty water into the air. Not many of the enemy were killed. They had smelled something coming and had pulled back into their rear trenches.

The Allied artillery raised its range at 5 A.M. and

began to lay down a rolling barrage. Behind the moving wall of explosions the first wave of Yanks went over the top. "No man's land," the space between the hostile armies, was blanketed with a heavy fog. The first wave of men disappeared into the mist as if their bodies had dissolved. Then the second, then the third wave of doughboys scrambled over their parapets and plodded onward into the murk.

The veteran 1st and 2d Divisions went over the top, along with another regular division, the 5th. With them went men who a few weeks before were perhaps selling magazines or picking cotton. The states of South Dakota, Nebraska, Arizona, New Mexico, Kansas and Colorado walked with their lads of the 89th Division. Texas tumbled forward in the mud with the 90th. Men of every state fixed bayonets with the Rainbow Division, the all-American 42nd. Backing them up and awaiting orders were men from Delaware and New Jersey in the 78th Division. So were the regulars of the 3rd.

To watch the day dawn, John Joseph Pershing climbed a hill near the American jump-off line. He shivered as a cold wind and drizzle beat about his ears. Once a general has issued his orders he is the

loneliest man in the army, next to the solitary private
in his foxhole. There isn't much he can do to change or
correct matters after the shooting starts.

"The sky over the battlefield, both before and after
dawn, was aflame," he saw. "Exploding shells, star
signals, and burning supply dumps and villages presented a scene picturesque and terrible."

When he came down off the hill, the time was 9 A.M.
The first columns of German prisoners began to shuffle
by. J.J.P. was joined by Secretary of War Newton D.
Baker. Little Mr. Baker was cheerfully excited. He
has been shot at—what a tale to tell when he got back
to Washington!

Reports started to trickle back from the thundering
front. All went well, Pershing heard. And, thank God,
losses were amazingly slight!

The advance plunged onward. Barbed-wire en-
tanglements failed to slow down the Yanks. Our combat engineers had blown up much of the wire with
sewer pipes full of dynamite. The doughboys carried
rolls of chicken wire which they spread over the top of
the barbed tangles; they tramped swiftly across such
bridges. The French engineers were astonished at our
rapid passage through the barbed wire. At first they

thought quite seriously that the Yanks' success depended on bigger feet and longer legs than their *poilus* had!

Only one American division, the 26th, pushed eastward against the Heights of the Meuse. The New Englanders had been tested at the Aisne-Marne and were good troops. They and some French units labored slowly up the rocky, wooded hills. This part of J.J.P.'s attack was minor compared to the smash of eight divisions against the southern face of St. Mihiel. However, air scouts brought news that the Germans had begun to pull back from the salient. Pershing phoned the 26th to hurry, to go all-out to capture the town of Vigneulles, the road junction at the center of St. Mihiel.

The weary New Englanders did their job by 2 A.M. of September 13. A brigade of the 1st Division linked up with them at daybreak. A soldier-reporter for the army newspaper, *The Stars and Stripes,* talked to the doughboys who shook hands in Vigneulles. They were too dog-tired "to have an awful lot of conversation to spare," he wrote.

The jaws of a trap seemed to have snapped on General von Gallwitz's men at Vigneulles. But Pershing had a sharp disappointment coming to him. We took only 15,000 prisoners and 450 guns at St. Mihiel, at the cost of 7,000 American casualties. The great bulk of the German army got away, mauled but still full of fight.

The reason for J.J.P.'s frustration was odd indeed. By pure chance he had struck just as the Germans were about to leave the salient! They gave up only the ground that they had been ordered previously to vacate by their High Command. Some cynical Allied writers laughed and said that St. Mihiel was "the sector where the Americans relieved the Germans."

The joke was unkind and, like most unkind things, was quite unfair. The Germans may have chosen to leave St. Mihiel of their own accord, but actually they were thrown out. The doughboys hustled the enemy so rudely that General Liggett's 1st Corps advanced eight times faster than J.J.P. had allowed. Many Yanks charged so impetuously, in fact, that they were blown to bits by the Allied guns supporting them!

General Dickman of our 4th Corps agreed with J.J.P. that the lively doughboys could have continued their drive if Foch had not limited it before it started. The French Marshal did not believe that green Yanks could crack Germany's steel shell, the Hindenburg Line, with one single blow.

General Liggett agreed with the Commander in Chief's reasoning. So did von Gallwitz, the German defender of St. Mihiel, when all the generals were on speaking terms after the war. Our First Army had much to learn, these officers felt. The doughboys were good, but not good enough—not yet. They might have broken their heads and hearts trying to pierce the Hindenburg Line without a pause after St. Mihiel.

The pause Foch ordered was not a pause for rest, however. Instead, the doughboys found themselves training harder than ever to get ready for the showdown battle of the entire war.

# 18
## The Big Push

*Tout le monde à la bataille!*

Marshal Foch coined this phrase that describes his strategy for finishing off the Kaiser. We might translate it, "Everybody get in and fight!" Certainly that plan won the war a year sooner than many people, including General Pershing, had expected.

If we imagine the Allied armies as a gigantic scythe, or pruning hook, we can picture what happened.

119

The vengeful little Belgian Army was the point of the curved blade. The British and French armies were the central arc of the hook. The A.E.F. formed the cutting edge nearest to the handle. The doughboys would attack first, followed at one-day intervals by the French, British and last the Belgians.

*Tout le monde à la bataille* covered a front of hundreds of miles. The Yank sector involved less than one-fourth of the lines. A hundred ding-dong battles added up to the total "big push." Over a million Americans kept their share of the fighting going without rest for forty-seven days.

To keep his promise to Marshal Foch, J.J.P moved his victorious First Army after St. Mihiel. Over 600,000 men had to side-slip behind French-held Verdun. They had to sort themselves out and come into a new line of battle sixty miles away. And most of the shifting had to be done at night.

The 600,000 doughboys did the almost impossible in one almost incredible week. They slop-slopped along just three muddy, jam-packed roads. They fell into ditches. They lost their way. They lost precious equipment. And, above all rain fell almost continuously. Doughboy tempers turned sour.

"What outfit's that, buddy?" a military traffic cop

might challenge a column trudging toward a cross-
roads.

All sorts of sarcasms would boom back—especially
after dark.

"The Forty-Eleventh Dental Replacements!" "Hun-
nert-and-One Ranch!" "Miss Ashby's Female Semi-
nary, Dismounted—and what's it *to* you, anyhow,
Buster?"

At least the M.P.s could tell that the men were
Americans. And in spite of mud, confusion, and more
or less friendly heckling, the First Army got into position on time.

The Meuse-Argonne campaign opened with a bel-
low and flash of heavy guns on September 26, 1918.
After three hours of cannonading, the first wave of
Yank shock troops plodded into the Argonne Forest.
This was "a tangled mass of trees and underbrush,"
but the poor trees soon became stripped poles in a
wilderness of burnt ruin. Camouflaged machine guns
riddled the doughboys from ambush. Big guns blasted
down at them from the hill of Montfaucon and the
Heights of the Meuse. Snipers hidden in treetops
picked off man after man struggling through the
bushes. The Americans faced the hardest natural
obstacles of all the Allied armies. And the rain of

121

Lorraine poured down onto the mud, mud, mud.

The Germans had a desperate strategy for the fall of 1918. The Imperial High Command had folded away their fond dreams of world conquest. Yet they still were sure they could win a stand-off. Let the Allies hurl men against the Hindenburg Line, the enemy reasoned. Let the men die by the thousands until Washington, Paris and London are sickened. Then the Allies would be certain to grant generous peace terms—anything, anything to end the horrible slaughter!

General Pershing believed his men could punch into Germany itself before the first snowfall. General Pétain doubted it. The A.E.F. would go about one-third of the way, he said, and he turned out to be right. J.J.P.'s "confidence in the capacity of his untried army," one military writer says, "was to founder on the rock of machine guns."

Even at the end of World War I the machine gun was king of the battlefield as it was in the beginning. Very few tanks could penetrate the dense forest to get at the murderous Maxims. Only an eight-to-one superiority in numbers kept the Americans advancing in spite of fearful losses.

From left to right across the front, our starting line-up was:

First the 77th Division from the sidewalks of New York. Then the 28th, Pennsylvania's "Iron" men. Next the men from Missouri and Kansas in the 35th, whose height had impressed J.J.P. Then the 91st from eight far-western states and Alaska. Then the 37th from Ohio. After them the 79th, more Pennsylvanians. Then the only regular division, the 4th. Next the 80th from Virginia, West Virginia and Pennsylvania. Last the Illinois 33rd. Three more divisions formed a reserve. Only a quarter of the lot ever had sniffed burnt gunpowder before.

Pershing's attack was no "blitz" or lightning bolt. It was like a steamroller—steady, powerful and relentless. J.J.P. was borrowing the tactics of General Ulysses Grant, from Grant's victorious Wilderness Campaign. They were as dismal and as crushingly effective in the French wilderness in 1918 as they had been in Virginia in 1865.

To the west two American divisions fought with the French Fourth Army. The regular 2nd and the Texans and Oklahomans of the 36th banged away at a place called Blanc Mont. Their local victory helped to force a general German retreat along a much wider sector of the *poilus'* front.

With the Fourth British Army were two more Yank divisions. The first Allied troops to crack a hole in the Hindenburg Line were Americans. The honor fell to National Guard divisions from New York, Tennessee and North and South Carolina. These, the 27th and 30th, under General George W. Read, spearheaded Field Marshal Lord Haig's assault on what had been called the impregnable Hindenburg Line. They captured a strange part of it, an underground canal near Bellicourt, on September 29.

The big mass of the foe facing the British on the northern plains fell back more rapidly than the fewer Germans attacked by Pershing's doughboys. The enemy's retreat in Flanders upset his whole strategy of "bleed the Allies white." The Kaiser called Prince Max of Baden to form a new cabinet. The new Chancellor of the German Empire immediately asked President Wilson to "arrange an armistice on land, by sea, and in the air." Diplomatic notes began to fly back and forth. But killing continued amidst the splintered trees of the Argonne Forest. And blood still colored the brooks running down from the Heights of the Meuse.

By October 12 half of our forty-two divisions in France were leap-frogging in and out of the swelling battle. So General Pershing formed the Second Army, A.E.F., and put it under General Robert Lee Bullard. General Hunter Liggett took over the First Army from J.J.P., who supervised both men. On October 14 both Armies were crunching onward. The American front had fanned out from twenty to ninety miles.

The brave doughboys were awkward at the business of war. Even J.J.P. sometimes botched matters. Toward the end of the Meuse-Argonne campaign, for instance, he sent the 1st Division racing pell-mell to capture Sedan. Our 42nd also was aiming at the city. Their race turned into comic opera when the regulars swooped down on "Rainbow" headquarters and took one of the 42nd's generals prisoner. His name was Douglas MacArthur.

General Liggett angrily stopped the childish tom-foolery. He ordered *all* of the eager Yanks to stand aside. A French corps crossed the Meuse and entered Sedan. The city had been the scene of France's humiliating whipping by the Germans in 1870. Hunter Liggett's tactful gesture saved much bad feeling all around.

# 19
# The Lost Battalion

One tale by itself spells out the suffering and triumph of the whole Meuse-Argonne campaign. It is the story of a battalion that got separated from the rest of the division and became known as the Lost Battalion.

The 77th Division was from the sidewalks of New York. Major Charles W. Whittlesey commanded an extra-big battalion from the 308th Regiment of the 77th, in all about 700 men. They jumped off in the attack of October 2 at dawn, and by nightfall they were "lost."

The battalion had lanced into a gap between two large bodies of enemy troops. When the Germans recovered from their surprise, they closed in behind the Yanks and held them fast. The men of the 308th could go neither forward nor backward. Although they were only a thousand yards ahead of their buddies of the 77th Division the Lost Battalion may as well have been on the moon.

Major Whittlesey ordered his troops to dig in along a little brook near a wrecked mill. Through no fault of Whittlesey's the low, exposed position was very poor. The Germans had first choice of the ground; they overlooked the Yanks from the woodsy hills roundabout. Soon lead and iron began falling on the besieged doughboys. Major Whittlesey sent another order to his captains and lieutenants.

"Our mission is to hold this position at all costs," he wrote. "Have this understood by every man in the command."

The Major reported his position to the 77th's headquarters by carrier pigeons. His bird messengers kept the Major from feeling isolated.

On the first day of the siege, German shells of many

calibers plastered the battalion. The New Yorkers kept their heads down. They checked their haversacks and canteens; there was one day's food but no water. That night volunteers refilled some of the canteens from the creek. Many of these gallant waterboys pitched dead into the stream from shots fired by enemy sentinels. But the Lost Battalion hung on.

On the second day German infantry charged the New Yorkers. The enemy rushed in close enough to heave grenades into the American rifle pits. Twice they were beaten back at the cost of many casualties on both sides. First-aid kits became scarce among the besieged. Doughboys crept about recovering some medicine and bandages from their dead comrades, but there were no doctors to treat the wounded. Torn, white-lipped men had to patch up themselves. Yet the Lost Battalion hung on.

On the third day the Yanks were thumped by a heavy American bombardment. The grateful Germans piled mortar shells on top of the blasting the New Yorkers took from their own guns. Major Whittlesey's last pigeon flew back to his headquarters to report the tragic mistake. Two wild assaults by German infantry again had to be repulsed. During the night the Major posted sentries to keep his thirst-crazed soldiers from going to their deaths down by the creek. By planning forays to the stream after dark, Whittlesey obtained a small ration of slimy water. But now food was entirely gone. Yet the Lost Battalion hung on.

On the fourth day the enemy rushed the shrinking circle once more. And once more he was stopped by rifle fire as well-aimed as it was fast. In the afternoon French artillery pounded the New Yorkers. The Germans co-operated by attacking in waves after the second horrible error by Allied guns. The deadly rifles turned back the enemy as usual. Several American pilots tried to drop food to their trapped buddies, but the parcels fell within the German lines instead. By now all food and medicine were gone among the besieged Americans. Their wounded had to bind their hurts with filthy woolen leg puttees. And all that night a cold rain fell on the sick and hungry men. Still the Lost Battalion hung on.

On the fifth day American artillery found the range for support of the battalion. Our pilots had seen the American position from the air and so were useful in reporting it. Yank shell fire broke up one attempt by the Germans to mass for a charge. But this cheering sight was canceled for the Lost Battalion when they

129

saw American planes drop another shower of supplies behind enemy lines. More men of the battalion died as Maxim guns methodically raked the little creekside fort from end to end. Still more died in yet another infantry attack that followed the machine-gunning. But the Lost Battalion hung on.

Meanwhile General Pershing made a decision. An "important factor that entered into the decision," he wrote, "was the predicament of the 'Lost Battalion.'" J.J.P. threw two divisions at the rear and left flank of the Germans defending the northern Argonne Forest. Here was the enemy's main force that had Whittlesey's men trapped. Thirty thousand Yanks struck hard to relieve pressure on New York's 77th Division, which could not free its Lost Battalion. The rescuers were the old "Bloody Buckets" of the 28th, as well as fresh troops from Georgia, Alabama and Tennessee in the 82nd Division. The 77th began to move northward again by the help of the Pennsylvanians and the Southerners.

On the sixth day of the siege of the Lost Battalion, a limping American approached from the German lines carrying a white flag. The doughboy had been wounded and taken prisoner, but was released to carry a message to Major Whittlesey from the German commander. Typed neatly, the message read:

"The bearer . . . has been charged against his will to carry this letter to the officer in charge of the battalion of the 77th Division . . . The suffering of your wounded men can be heard over here in the German lines. We are appealing to your humane sentiments to stop. A white flag will tell us you agree. Please treat [the bearer of this letter] as an honorable man. He is quite a soldier. We envy you."

Whittlesey might have replied, "Nuts!" to the Germans, as another American officer did under similar circumstances during World War II. But the Major ignored the message. Well, not quite. Instead of answering, Whittlesey took in the two white sheets he had laid out on the ground to mark his position for Allied planes. He did not want these white markers to be mistaken by the Germans for surrender signals. The stubborn Major had no intention of giving up.

His silence gave the German commander no choice but to attack. This he did with everything he had, including flame throwers. Masses of gray-clad men charged, yelling, shooting, spraying fire and hurling grenades. The Lost Battalion stolidly mowed them down until they retreated. But when dusk fell the lot of the defenders was pitiable indeed.

Only two useless machine guns remained of Whittlesey's original nine. All his gunners were dead. Wounded men were manning the trenches; twice-wounded men had been reloading their hot rifles for them. However, most of their ammunition was gone by now. Only bayonets and clubbed rifles were left to beat off the enemy. In the darkness the exhausted men snapped on their bayonets. They knew what would happen. The next attack would be the last, for the Germans would wipe them out. But the Lost Battalion would hang on to the end.

No attack came. During the night the enemy vanished. The slashing of the 28th and 82nd Divisions at his flank had gotten on the enemy's nerves. The 77th was able to move ahead and free their "lost" buddies.

Just 194 men out of Whittlesey's original 700 could walk—and some of these were badly wounded. They met their friends of the 77th with a grumpy question: "What kept you?"

Major Whittlesey won the Congressional Medal of Honor for a remarkable bulldog defense of a remarkably unimportant acre of the Argonne Forest. But the siege of the Lost Battalion proved one really important thing. And that was that an American soldier could be as disciplined and steadfast as any fighting man in the world.

This proof was a triumph for John Joseph Pershing. The sidewalks of New York are no place to raise expert riflemen, as the mountains and prairies traditionally have been. Yet the murderous marksmanship of the Lost Battalion had crumbled every German attack. The New Yorkers had not been born crack shots, no. But they had learned to shoot while they learned to salute. And they had gained confidence in themselves and their officers while they had been shining buttons!

Pershing was disliked as a martinet by many men of the A.E.F. But the cool General knew that the stubborn stand of his Lost Battalion would discourage the enemy. Boys from Manhattan, Queens, Brooklyn, Richmond and the Bronx had shown the Kaiser that the American Army was no mere mob of dumb Johns.

# 20
## The Pyramid of Honor

A patrol from Company G was being shot to smither-
eens in a forlorn pocket of the Argonne Forest. Only
one non-commissioned officer and seven men were left.
The doughboys were pinned down by a hot sleet of
machine-gun bullets. These were men of the 82nd Division who were trying to help the 77th and its Lost
Battalion. Now their own ammunition was almost

gone and they were tired, bewildered and frightened. To make matters worse they had to watch a batch of German prisoners they had captured.

The surviving non-commissioned officer of Company G's patrol was a lean, red-faced, red-haired corporal. Flat on his belly, he squinted over a log. The land ahead was rough, wooded and hilly, just like the part of Tennessee where he had been born. Corporal Alvin C. York hadn't wanted to leave Tennessee to become a soldier. He hated feudin' and fightin'. Such goings-on were sinful, he believed. Alvin nearly had wound up in a camp for "conshies," or conscientious objectors to military service. Eventually an infantry captain argued Alvin into carrying a rifle.

Stuttering explosions burst out in front of Alvin's protecting log. He pulled in his long neck. But Alvin's green eyes had spotted the machine gun's position, and he determined to get it.

Corporal York crawled away alone into the forest. He was a hunter from birth. Back home in the wilderness of the Cumberland plateau, he had learned how to creep up on wild turkeys. Now he was stalking bigger game. But hunting would be pretty much the same in these Frenchy woods as it was in Tennessee, Alvin reckoned.

He heard a rustle and saw a movement in the bushes. He froze. Then Alvin recognized a "coal scuttle" helmet—a German! Corporal York soundlessly raised his rifle, drew a bead and squeezed off one shot. The wearer of the big helmet lurched and fell on his face. Corporal York crawled on.

He wriggled to forest cover where he could ambush the German machine gun. Alvin had no cartridges to waste. So he aimed only one bullet to a customer and soon the Maxim gun fell as silent as its dead crew. Corporal York reloaded and crawled on. Again and again he bushwhacked the enemy, like Cumberland turkeys. Careless Germans by ones, by twos and by groups fell to Alvin's unerring rifle.

The enemy began to realize that something unseen and fearful was lurking in the underbush. Their own guns made so much racket that they drowned the cracks of Alvin's lone rifle. Yet a German might turn to speak to his *kamerad* (comrade) only to discover the man was dead without apparent cause. Terror gripped the Germans. Their officers shouted for them to be calm. But officers, too, were dying from the death that crept in the green woods.

Corporal York thought that German hunting was easier than squirrel hunting. Well, squirrels didn't have machine guns, of course. But then these foreigners weren't as smart as Tennessee squirrels, either.

Suddenly the noisy forest fell quiet. In the hush a German voice called out in English. Alvin saw something white and dirty flutter from behind a tree. An undershirt it was, or maybe a cleaner pair of drawers than Alvin had worn for weeks. The guttural voice shouted that his men wanted to give up to the American regiment that had them surrounded.

"The American regiment" yelped for his squad to come help him. And no wonder! The woods erupted with Germans waving their hands and crying, *"Kamerad!"* in token of surrender. Corporal York's patrol turned over their unwanted *kamerads* to the very nearest American headquarters. The officers there rubbed their eyes when the gray parade of Germans walked by, unarmed and downcast. Later on, when the officers were poking about in the forest, they still could not believe what they saw.

Single-handed, Alvin C. York had captured four German officers and 128 men! And sprawled dead among the trees were twenty-four more of the foe, each with a single bullet in him!

The American headquarters telephoned the commander of Alvin's regiment, the 328th Infantry. Had he heard about his man York? No, said the colonel of the 328th—what about York? He hadn't received a report concerning Company G's patrol.

Corporal York of Fentress County, Tennessee, U.S.A., had gone to sleep without telling a soul about his German-hunting. He was just too all-fired-tired, that's why!

Besides winning the Congressional Medal the Corporal won the third stripe of a sergeant. A newspaper reporter accidentally discovered something that scared the hero. When the newspaper man asked Alvin if he was married, Alvin turned beet-red.

"Well no," stammered Sergeant York. "I was always kind of a mommer's boy."

Four days after Sergeant York's exploit, a man named Samuel Woodfill also won the Congressional Medal of Honor. Sam was broad-chested and six feet tall, although his even-bigger family back home considered him their runt. Lieutenant Woodfill commanded a company of the 60th Infantry in the Argonne. This Indiana boy was the kind of officer who hated to see his men get hurt.

Woodfill's division, the 5th, was punching at Cunel on October 12, 1918. The ground was hilly, and the going almost as hard as at Montfaucon. The Germans resisted with the fury of despair. The *Amerikaners* were drawing very near to the untouched soil of the German fatherland itself. Too many of Sam's men had crumpled and died under the German fury, he thought—if he thought at all.

Big Sam saw red. His chewed-up company was stopped, hugging the earth under a machine gun's fire. So Sam borrowed a rifle and squirmed on his belly toward the chattering Maxim. Ten yards away a gunner glimpsed Sam and barked a warning. Four foolhardy Germans rushed Lieutenant Woodfill to take him prisoner. Sam calmly plugged three with his borrowed rifle and tackled the fourth, an officer, hand to hand. The two men kicked, punched and bit each other until Sam was able to jerk his pistol free and fire it.

Lieutenant Woodfill blew his whistle and waved his men onward. Again a spray of bullets halted them. This time Sam wasted no strength in crawling. He ran straight at the machine gun nest, pausing only to kneel and shoot. Three gunners were dead from his attack when he burst into the nest. The survivors threw up their hands—"*Kamerad!*" Sam angrily wrecked their Maxim with his rifle and kept them cowed until his company caught up with them.

The Yanks staggered on. For a third time they hit the dirt under the *rat-tat-tat* of Maxim lead. And for the third time mighty Sam, the one-man army, lunged into action. With rifle shots he killed five of the gun crew. Then he pulled his Colt .45 to charge the rest. They fled.

Another gun near by swung around and peppered him. Sam veered and rushed his second nest of the past two minutes. On the brink of the machine gun's pit, Sam's pistol gave out. He threw it at the startled Germans and grabbed a pickax he saw lying near by. This ugly weapon was the finish of the last two enemy gunners.

The motto of Samuel Woodfill's regiment is "To the Utmost Extent of Our Power." For Sam this meant to the utmost extent of three rifles, a pistol, a pickax, and his fists, feet, and teeth!

The deeds of the A.E.F. won the Congressional Medal for ninety-five of its troops. In 1918 more decorations for outstanding service were adopted to supplement the Medal of Honor. General Pershing encouraged the erection of "the Pyramid of honor," the unofficial phrase describing the 1918 Act. Congressional Medal of Honor men stood at the peak of the pyramid, the bravest of the brave. Next came the winners of the Distinguished Service Cross, then the Distinguished Service Medal, then the Silver Star, and so on down the widening pyramid. Some of these medals may be earned by civilians as well as soldiers and sailors, including the second highest, the Distinguished Service Cross.

The broad, solid base of the pyramid of honor was not cemented until February 22, 1932. Then Congress admitted thousands of veterans to the fellowship of the Purple Heart. This decoration was sent to men who had been wounded during World War I, or to the families of men who died. It was no accident that the Purple Heart was re-established on Washington's birthday. He had devised the award back during the American Revolution.

Heroes do not come in certain sizes, nor do they wear certain emblems of rank. Neither does color of skin nor place of birth have anything to do with the making of a hero. America was proud to present the

Congressional Medal to aliens in the A.E.F. who came from Italy, England, Norway, Greece, Austria, Ireland, Finland, Holland, and what is now Yugoslavia.

More privates won the Congressional Medal than lieutenants. More sergeants won the award than all the top brass combined. And no general of the A.E.F. won it during World War I. Does this mean that doughboys are braver than their officers? Not necessarily. There are more of them, for one thing. And they get more opportunities to show conspicuous gallantry "above and beyond the call of duty."

A belated winner of our country's highest decoration received his on November 11, 1921. Neither the soldier's mother nor his wife attended the ceremony, but the President of the United States did. Probably none of the soldier's buddies turned out for the parade. But many high dignitaries of Europe paid him honor dressed in shiny top hats and red sashes. The soldier himself could not see the Stars and Stripes waving over the quiet hills at Arlington, Virginia. Nor could he hear the speeches and the crash of musketry that saluted him.

The soldier's family was not there because they could not be invited. His doughboy buddies were not there because they did not recognize him. But the whole world could be notified who he was, and *you* know him.

He is the Unknown Soldier.

# 21
## Knights of the Wild Blue Yonder

Combat in the skies began almost comically. The first pilots in 1914 were unarmed. Enemy fliers usually ignored one another but might wave hello to an enemy they came to recognize. Then one day an unknown enthusiast took a pistol up into the clouds with him. Before you could say "Wright brothers!" every pilot was flying with a rifle across his knees—or even with a bag

144

of bricks at his feet. French fliers actually downed two German planes by throwing bricks!

Another Frenchman learned how to shoot a machine gun straight through his whirling propeller. A Dutchman working for the Germans, Anthony Fokker, invented a better way to do the same thing. (After the war Fokker became an American citizen.) Pilots tried wrenching twists, turns and loops to "get on the tail" of an enemy. A biplane's wings might fall off in mid-air with the strains, but the pioneer pilots just had to experiment. Tactics sprang up, too, including flying and fighting in V-formation instead of singly and helter-skelter.

Bombing pilots did little in World War I. The high "brass" did not know how to use bombers. The limelight shone on the fighter pilots—Guynemer and Fonck of France, Richthofen and Udet of Germany, Mannock and Bishop of the British Empire, and Luke and Rickenbacker of the United States. These were leading aces. An "ace" was, and still is, a pilot who officially destroys five enemy planes.

Air fighting was a graceful, murderous ballet. Compared to the brutal slugging match going on down in the reeking trenches, it was fairly unimportant. Wars

still could be won on the ground in 1914-1918. However, the newness of battle above the clouds stirred
everyone's imagination. Aerial dogfights were like the
jousting between the fabulous Knights of the Round
Table. And some of the early Knights of the Wild Blue
Yonder were mighty champions, indeed.

A few were "cool pilots," like Lieutenant René
Fonck and Baron Manfred von Richthofen. The
Frenchman scored seventy-five victories (some say
126), yet seldom had to patch a bullet hole in his
wings. The German racked up eighty kills while he
methodically planned and tested new fighting tech-
niques. On the other hand, Bishop of Canada and
Guynemer of France were "hot pilots." The Canadian
flew with "savage elation," painting his plane bright
blue so that no German could mistake whose it was.
Billy Bishop downed seventy-two enemies. The
"Miraculous Georges" Guynemer's plane always
landed full of bullet holes because of his reckless
manner of fighting. Once when his ammunition was
gone, the Frenchman deliberately rammed his foe
head-on in the sky and somehow survived! Georges
was a sickly little fellow, but he got fifty-three Germans before they finally got him.

American adventurers rose into the dogfights over France in 1916. Seven Yanks, some from the Foreign Legion, formed the "Lafayette Escadrille." By the time the United States entered the war, over three hundred Americans had flown with the Escadrille and had made it France's third best squadron. Raoul Lufbery and James Norman Hall, two of the Escadrille's aces, became instructors for the baby American squadrons in 1918. Lufbery was killed, but Hall lived to write *Mutiny on the Bounty* and many other popular books after the guns fell silent.

"On April 1, 1918," General Pershing reported, "we had only one aero squadron in action—my old squadron of the Mexican Punitive Expedition." Not until May did the American fliers receive English machine guns for their French fighter planes. But our Air Service climbed into the skies over Château-Thierry and at the Aisne-Marne. There were twenty-one squadrons by July 15, some with victories and losses on their records. Teddy Roosevelt's youngest son, Quentin, plunged to his death in a dogfight over Château-Thierry.

Among the first Yank aviators to take to the air under his own flag was an Ohioan named Edward V.

147

Rickenbacker. He knew gasoline engines as few pilots did, for Eddie had been a racing-car driver back home. He volunteered to fly in France and found himself driving a car instead. The man he drove around was none other than John Joseph Pershing.

Eddie's job as J.J.P.'s chauffeur proved to be a short cut to the skies. He became America's ace of aces with twenty-six victories. Like Fonck and Richthofen, Eddie Rickenbacker was a "cool pilot." He was a big, slow man with steady nerves whose motto was, "It never pays to take an *unnecessary* risk." The progress of aviation during our times owes much to this principle, in peace even more than in war. Planes ceased being "toys" and "just good sport" when men studied them seriously. Captain Rickenbacker came home after the war to make automobiles and later on became president of a big air line.

The exact opposite of Eddie was a stocky, blond fellow from Arizona. Frank Luke was "eager, reckless, boastful, critical of his superiors, loose in his talk, and decidedly fresh." Plainly he was hard to get along with. But this wild Westerner had no fear whatsoever. Danger made Frank laugh aloud. His German-killing career lasted only two weeks—but in that incredibly short time he burned twenty-one enemy aircraft out of the sky!

The only real friend the cocky Arizonan had was a quiet man from Boston named Joe Wehner. Joe's German birth had caused both American and French police to arrest him three times while he was in uniform—*American* uniform. Joe might have resigned in disgust, but he stuck out the humiliations. Courage often means more than heroism, and Joe Wehner had that kind of courage.

The strange team of Luke and Wehner chose observation balloons for their prey. German planes were getting scarce in September, 1918, and Luke was restless with nothing to shoot at. Now, balloons were the toughest targets of all—make no mistake about that! Not a dozen pilots from all the armies combined ever became aces for knocking balloons out of the air. Only three of these lived to tell their stories after the war. The reason was that a flier had to aim his plane straight down into the muzzles of the antiaircraft cannon and machine guns that ringed every balloon.

Frank and Joe double-teamed the gas bags. Joe "sat upstairs" to prevent German pilots from getting on

Frank's tail. Joe became an ace just batting enemies away from his buddy's rear! Frank would dive steeply right into the storm of shells, tracers, and "flaming onions" of phosphorus protecting the balloon. Lieutenant Luke thought the gaudy colors of the fountain of death coming at him were beautiful. "Like Roman candles or Fourth of July flowerpots," he said.

On the day Joe Wehner was killed, Frank Luke avenged him by shooting down two balloons and three Fokker planes in the blazing time of seven minutes flat! As usual he returned to his base unhurt. But his Spad fighter was ragged with punctures—one hole straight up through the seat. Frank was puzzled trying to guess why that bullet had not ended in *his* seat.

How do you imagine this wild and woolly Westerner died? He met his death while he was A.W.O.L. —absent without leave! Frank had taken off in his plane and stayed away overnight without permission, as he did too often. If Lieutenant Luke had returned from his last patrol, he would have been court-martialed.

There are sworn witnesses to Frank's last feats of "balloon busting." Many citizens of the little village of Murvaux saw everything. Frank's Spad fighter plane was hit by eight Fokkers that were chasing him. Quite possibly this gang had been searching the clouds especially for the terrible balloon buster, as Frank was called. He dived to treetop level to escape his tormentors, badly wounded and with a sputtering engine. A little way off were three German balloons. Frank streaked toward them close to the ground and sent all three flaming down in three minutes. With his last bullets he gunned German infantry in Murvaux, killing six soldiers. Then he crashed.

Lieutenant Luke was hurt and thirsty. He limped toward a brook near the wreck of his Spad. A patrol of Germans cut him off. Frank would not surrender. He fired his pistol at the riflemen until he dropped with a bullet through his heart. He was just twenty years old, this fierce warrior of the wild blue yonder.

American aviation got only a mild push from World War I. Colonel William Mitchell, chief of our Air Service, had a mere 200 American-made planes under his command when the war ended. Colonel Billy Mitchell argued and protested after the war that planes would be decisive in future clashes between nations. In fact the far-seeing Colonel made so much noise that his superiors ordered him to shut up. Billy Mitchell did not, was court-martialed for insubordination and was convicted.

Time went by, and time proved that Billy Mitchell was right. So the stain of his conviction was wiped out, and the Colonel was promoted to General. It would have been nicer if Billy Mitchell had been around to hear such good news. But he had been dead a number of years by the time he was promoted and honored.

# 22

## The Dining Car in the Forest

The German cause fell like a mighty tower. First it trembled slightly, then slowly tilted and finally toppled with a rush and a roar. The United States lent a powerful shove to the final grand smash.

Yanks helped in a small way even in places seldom mentioned today. For instance, the 332d Regiment of the 83rd Division, Buckeyes from Ohio, fought shoulder to shoulder with the Italians. Their enemies were

Austrians along the north bank of the Piave River above Venice. On November 4 after the ten-day Battle of Vittorio Veneto, the Austrian army was utterly crushed. The Austro-Hungarian Empire sued for peace. General Armando Diaz's Italians won sweet revenge for their earlier defeat at Caporetto.

Even where none of the fresh Americans was fighting, triumph came to the Allies. Greeks, British, French, Serbs and Italians formed a hodgepodge army in the Balkans. They faced a similarly mixed force of Bulgarians, Germans and Austrians. On September 15 the Serbs smote the center of the enemy in Macedonia, ancient home of Alexander the Great. The Bulgarians and Austrians cracked, and their line split in two. Fifteen days later Bulgaria surrendered. Again there was a fine taste of revenge, this time for the Serbs. Serbia had been the first victim of the war.

In the Holy Land victory also came to the English, Australians, New Zealanders and British Indians. They had been opposing the ill-equipped but indomitable Turks, allies of Germany. Arab raiders on camels, led by a mysterious Briton named T.E. Lawrence, had hacked and dynamited behind the Turkish lines. Battle dispatches from Palestine carried place names that were hoary with antiquity. Civilians read news of maneuvers around the River Jordan, the Sea of Galilee, Jerusalem and Jericho. New invaders from Europe stormed Turkish strongholds at Aleppo and Acre, as in the old days of the Knights Crusaders. Turkish-German headquarters at the Battle of Megiddo in 1918 were located in Nazareth, boyhood home of Jesus. Gradually the tough Turks softened. On October 31 the Turks cried out, "Enough!" and signed papers taking them out of the war.

Even the continent of Africa echoed with gunfire. Lions, elephants, giraffes—all fled in panic at the sound of a thunder they could not understand. British South African troops and Germans ambushed one another in the jungles, on the grassy *veldts* and atop lonely mountains. The forces engaged were tiny, but their hardships were enormous. The African skirmishes followed a trail 3500 miles long!

One by one, Germany's partners on other fronts were dropping away in the fall of 1918.

Meanwhile in Europe German armies were crumbling. On the American front our First Army broke out of the worst of the terrible rocks and trees through which they had been plunging. On November 1 the Yanks began pounding northward across rolling land toward the German border. Town after town fell to their relentless push. The deadly Maxim guns and new types of poison gas failed to halt the rush. Nor did a natural scourge that was punishing all combatants. Germans and Allies alike died of influenza, a disease which remains a treacherous killer to this day.

Only eighteen tanks went along to cope with the Maxim gun nests. General Pershing said, "It seems strange that, with the American genius for manufacturing iron and steel, we should find ourselves . . . almost completely without these mechanical contrivances. . . ." However, a helping hand stretched out to the doughboys from the United States Navy. Three batteries of giant 14-inch battleship guns mounted on railway carriages joined the final drive of the First Army. These 117-ton monsters heaved death and ruin onto enemy supply roads miles away.

By November 7 the Germans were almost running before the First Army. J.J.P. sensed that victory was near. The General urged his men to push onward without bothering to keep abreast of one another. He even allowed trucks to run with bright headlights at night, without fear of drawing German fire. Our Second Army also was grinding out mileage, but it was the hammer blows of the First that sprung open the gates to Germany. "The results obtained by this Army have been felt on the entire front from the Moselle (River) to Holland," General Pershing announced. The Germans opposite the French and British swung shakily back like a door whose hinge has been cracked. The enemy in Lorraine, pounded by the First Army, had been their hinge.

In Germany itself, life was in turmoil. Imperial Navy sailors had mutinied in Kiel and Hamburg, beginning a revolution that hastened the end. Marshal von Hindenburg dismissed his commander in the west, von Ludendorff. But the internal revolt spread, and soldiers joined it. Barricades of paving stones and furniture finally rose in Berlin's streets. Armed clerks, still clad in neat business suits complete with hats and neckties, crouched behind the barricades beside soldiers, sailors and factory hands.

On November 10 his Imperial German Majesty, Kaiser Friedrich Wilhelm Viktor Albert von Hohenzollern, ran for his life into neutral Holland. With him trailed his family and his pet dachshunds. The Kaiser had lost his splendid armies and banners forever. He had lost his crown and estates too. In Holland he learned how to saw wood to keep busy.

The German armistice committee had crossed the

Allied lines on November 7 to talk to Marshal Foch. President Woodrow Wilson had refused to deal with the Kaiser. Instead he told the German government to cleanse itself and become truly representative of the German people. If Germany merely wanted a cease-fire agreement, its generals must talk to Foch. A genuine peace treaty would come later.

The Commander in Chief, Foch, made his head-quarters in a railroad dining car. General Pershing had been using one as his field office too. But at the time the armistice was signed, Pershing's car was at Trèves, miles away from Foch's. So J.J.P. did not witness the formal end of the war.

The Commander in Chief's wooden diner, side-tracked in a forest near Compiègne, France, bore the number 2419D. The bitter German officers must have made a note of that number during their four days of pleading with Foch. Years later, in 1940, the then-victorious Germans hauled old 2419D out of retirement. They forced the French to sign a surrender in it to wipe out the blot of 1918. Afterwards Adolf Hitler, the dictator of Nazi Germany, jigged a dance of joy outside the railroad car.

World War I closed at eleven A.M. of the eleventh day of the eleventh month, 1918. The figure one appears here at the end of John Joseph Pershing's fighting career as it had in the beginning.

A hush fell on the battlefields after the bugles blew at eleven o'clock that chilly November morning. As noon drew on, the loudest sounds were the clinking of mess kits and the coughing of men with colds. The twittering of birds could be heard for the first time in months. Some soldiers seized the heaven-sent chance to take baths. A crust had formed on their skins under uniforms they'd fought and slept in for weeks. Other doughboys were more suspicious. Was the unpleasantness, as they cynically called the war, really over? These doubting Thomases stripped and cleaned their rifles rather than themselves. The armistice might be just another trench rumor.

Indeed, one Yank apparently did not trust his luck until he had boarded a ship for home a few weeks later. As the French shore receded, his face lit up. Then he blew a kiss toward the land.

"*Au revoir,* Lafayette—here we go!" shouted the happy doughboy.

General Pershing began to lay plans for the American share in the Army of Occupation. Some divisions of doughboys would have to cross the "sacred" Rhine River into Germany soon. So Pershing buckled down to work again. To tell the truth, he took a rather dim view of the Armistice. John Joseph Pershing, like Ulysses S. Grant, wanted an unconditional surrender and not a mere truce. But he and the British commander, Lord Haig, gave way to the wishes of the French.

With his own eyes J.J.P. later saw the quiet, unscarred lands of Germany. He could not help contrasting them with the savagely torn fields of France. Pershing did not want to blacken and blast the country of his ancestors, mark you. He simply felt that the German people did not realize that they had been licked. A total surrender might have thumped that home to them. The milder armistice terms even allowed German regiments to parade back home, rifles in hand and flags flying.

Perhaps J.J.P. was right. Certainly no real peace followed World War I, as we all have learned to our great sorrow.

# 23

## A Long Armistice

"Your deeds will live forever on the most glorious pages of America's history." So spoke John Joseph Pershing to his A.E.F. the day after the war ended. Twenty months before November 11, 1918, J.J.P. was hoping for a million men by May. The United States was not able to ship them on time. However, a million men *returned* to the United States by May, 1919.

And the million left in Europe could hardly wait their turns.

More than 115,000 doughboys lay dead beneath the French earth. Many lie there still in cemeteries planned by J.J.P. And more than a quarter of a million of the A.E.F. brought home scars and wounds, some of which never healed. Our joy as a nation was clouded by our losses.

The splintered trees of the Argonne Forest put forth new leaves in the spring. French peasants plowed their fields warily, knowing that some farmers would be blown to bits by unexploded, buried shells. The green grass crept back to cover the trenches, and meadow larks and rabbits cheerily returned to their homes in the grass. Refugee French children began to learn how to play unafraid.

Yet there was no peace on earth and little good will toward men anywhere. As time went on, we in America were shaken by doubts. World War I and its purposes seemed deceitful. Some men have called the decade of the 1920s "the age of disillusion," meaning a time of doubting ideals. The fine spirit of making the world "safe for democracy" drew weary laughs from former soldiers, writers, politicians and just plain people.

What had happened to us?

For one thing we had learned that our Allies had agreed privately during the war to loot the empires of their enemies after victory. Decent Americans were shocked that any Allied nation could be so ignoble as to fight for profit rather than for principle. President Wilson was one who protested. The first of his Fourteen Points was aimed at outlawing such secret skulduggery. Treaties should be "open covenants . . . openly arrived at," said Woodrow Wilson.

Wilson presented his Fourteen Points in person at the Palace of Versailles, near Paris, on January 18, 1919. No President in our history until then had traveled beyond our borders while in office. The French people mobbed him with love and honors. But Wilson's eagerness to work abroad for his ideas cost him dearly at home. Our Senate finally rejected the Treaty of Versailles.

Wilson fought for a peace treaty that *guaranteed* peace. His Fourteen Points demanded open treaties, fewer trade barriers, freedom of the seas, less spending for armies, and fair settlement of boundary disputes. The most important Point was Number Fourteen, a plan for a League of Nations.

He was ahead of his time. Not until the United Nations was launched in 1945 did our United States accept Woodrow Wilson's thinking.

President Wilson stubbornly refused to split his League of Nations plank from the rest of the Versailles Treaty. A political dogfight broke out in Washington that ended in defeat—and death—for a great President. Woodrow Wilson fought so hard for his principles that he collapsed. A paralytic stroke laid him low, and he never recovered.

The diplomats of the triumphant Allies at Versailles chopped away much of Wilson's Fourteen Points. The air in the palace was smoky with revenge and distrust. There was no breathing space for idealism. On June 28 German representatives were summoned to the palace's beautiful Hall of Mirrors. They were handed pen and ink and ordered, "Sign here!"

The treaty forced Germany to confess sole guilt for World War I. She lost Alsace-Lorraine to France and other lands to Denmark, Poland and Belgium. Her African colonies were torn away and parceled out among the victors. She was ordered to pay for damage done during the four years of war. The Germans protested and argued, but squeezed few concessions from the Allies. The hard grudges begun by the treaty boded no good for the future.

Other treaties punished Austria-Hungary, Bulgaria and Turkey by sawing off pieces of their territories. In the case of Austria-Hungary the cutting was complete; the ancient domain of the Hapsburg emperors disappeared. Nine new or re-born nations were assembled from the pieces taken from Germany and her allies. Even Russia was hacked. Sorely weakened by defeat and revolution, she could not resist.

The badly fitting jigsaw puzzle of Europe in the 1920s pleased practically nobody. Lost territories, discontent and hunger speeded the rise of cruel dictators who terrorized the world for the next generation—Hitler of Germany, Stalin of Soviet Russia, and Mussolini of Italy. The Treaty of Versailles proved to be no peace treaty but rather a guarantee of more wars. Many historians call the time after 1918, even up to our own day, "the long armistice." Meaning just a truce between armed camps or a pause between rounds.

As the postwar years of the 1920s passed by, we discovered to our disgust that our recent Allies disliked us. Partly this hard feeling sprang from jealousy; the United States was an unchallenged world power now. But much of the feeling boiled around war debts. European cartoonists drew a fat Uncle Sam lounging on bags of money soaked in blood. We had lent tools, goods and capital to the world—only to learn that nobody loves a money-lender.

With the sole exception of Finland our debtors failed to meet their payments. Germany also fell behind on payments of war damages to the Allies. The Germans argued that 33 billions of dollars was too heavy a load. Yet the same nation raised far vaster sums to wage a second war bigger than World War I. An evil genius named Adolf Hitler was to show how Germany could shoulder a burden for war, if not for peace.

# 24
## They Just Fade Away

The politicians of America thought that John J. Pershing, the war hero, would make a splendid candidate for President of the United States. But J.J.P. flatly refused to enter politics.

"My country trained me as a soldier. I have had the fortune to lead its army to victory. That is enough."

He stuck to his decision. Possibly Pershing was influenced by the sorry fate of another fine general who

167

became President, Ulysses S. Grant. J.J.P. behaved more like the South's hero, Robert E. Lee, than like the man of the North who had won our Civil War. Pershing even refused to become a director or president of any industry. Many large business firms would have paid him handsomely to do absolutely nothing. Just to be able to print the famous name on their stationery would have been enough.

However, Pershing was grateful to be named General of the Armies of the United States. This was honor a-plenty for "a soldier who wished only to be a soldier." No other man ever has held the rank.

J.J.P. took charge of our small peacetime army in 1921 as Chief of Staff, retiring in 1924. Colonel George C. Marshall was his aide. During this time Pershing also planned the work of the Battle Monuments Commission, making many trips abroad to revisit battlefields and former comrades-in-arms like Pétain and Foch. In between times he worked on his book, *My Experiences in the World War*.

The two-volume book is not easy to read, for it is not charged with electric English. But no "ghost" wrote Pershing's book. "There is the record," he said, with the satisfaction of a man who did things for himself. The Pulitzer Prize judges decided that his *Experiences* were worthy of the History Award when the book was published in 1931.

We have a picture of J.J.P. then from an editor who visited the General in his Washington office to discuss his manuscript. The young publisher's man wore the ribbon of the Distinguished Service Cross in his buttonhole. The old man noticed the ribbon—"as he was supposed to," says the editor, "although I didn't usually flaunt it around."

"How did you get that?" asked Pershing.

"Oh, I was lucky," said George Shively. "Someone was kind."

Pershing snorted. "No one got that in the A.E.F. unless he deserved it!" he snapped. Then he listened to the story behind the ribbon that is second only to the Congressional Medal. Pershing may have recognized the story because he had read carefully the citations for all the high-ranking medals. Pershing won the D.S.C. himself for his daring at Mount Bogsak in the Philippines, long after the event.

Shively remembers that the white-haired Pershing "didn't act like the granite statue he was supposed to be. He was cordial. His occasional gruffness did not

169

conceal a twinkling of humor back of the keen blue eyes." This was John Joseph Pershing at the age of seventy. A rather lonely old man living at his Washington club who hated parties but who still loved to dance! "He was not displeased that a charming young woman should find him a welcome partner, especially if she danced well," a friend says.

J.J.P. gave up dancing and horseback riding as his years grew heavier. Eventually he made his home at Walter Reed Hospital in Washington. A new war broke out in Europe. As J.J.P. had warned, the Germans never really believed that they had been fairly beaten in World War I. A new A.E.F. had to go "over there" again to prove that Germany's first licking had been no fluke.

The old General stayed home, of course. But he was proud when Warren, his only son, enlisted as a private in the new A.E.F. Warren marched with his father's beloved First Army from Normandy's beachhead to Berlin, ending his service as a major. Battle reports from France must have stirred memories in the mind of the old soldier at home. Pershing had known many of the places very well.

Came a day when J.J.P. turned eighty, and our

newspapers ran notices about him: "Pershing Gravely Ill," and "Hero of Kaiser's War Sinking Fast." But there is a verse the army sings to a Sunday School tune that fitted John Joseph Pershing:

> *Old soldiers never die, never die, never die,*
> *Old soldiers never die, they just fade away.*

When he faded away quietly in 1948, the old soldier had seen eighty-eight years go by. Pershing lived to hear that his country had defeated its enemies in another worldwide war. His thoughts turned in wonder over the menace of atomic warfare. How swiftly the globe had spun since his birth before the Civil War! Gone were the days of galloping horse cavalry. Gone were the raiding Indians. Gone even were the uses of a mass army like his old A.E.F. Yes, life changed always, and all life was full of wonders.

Two Presidents and a President-to-be followed the General's coffin to pay him the last respects his country could show him. One was Herbert Hoover, the young man of 1917 who had preached that "Food Will Win the War." Another was Harry S. Truman, a fellow Missourian, and an artillery captain in Pershing's

A.E.F. The third man was Dwight D. Eisenhower, a general who was to become a President.

There is one tale left to tell. Perhaps it will remind you a bit of a young Lieut of many years ago—the Lieut who clicked back into his tent on the parade ground of the University of Nebraska.

The time was the disastrous year of 1940. France had fallen before the might of a German onslaught. The dining car with the number 2419D had sheltered the victors and vanquished in roles reversed from 1918. J.J.P.'s close friend, Marshal Philippe Pétain, was trying to pick up the pieces of his broken country. Pershing grieved for his old comrade, we know.

Suddenly a summons came for the aged General who rested half-forgotten in his rooms at Walter Reed Hospital. President Franklin D. Roosevelt wished to consult with J.J.P. A newspaperman recalls Pershing's visit to the White House very clearly.

"He came on one of those hot, steamy Washington days," Ray Brecht says. "We reporters were hanging around in the lobby of the President's Executive Offices, hoping for news that would cheer us up. The disaster in France had us all feeling pretty bad."

Then the outline of a man appeared in the doorway.

Bright sunshine silhouetted his square shoulders. "We ought to have known by *that* who the old man was," says Brecht. "Pershing never slouched."

The newspapermen gathered around the General. He posed for pictures but refused to answer any questions. Smiling, he excused himself. "The President has called me, gentlemen," J.J.P. said. "I must not keep him waiting."

The reporters could tell that the eighty-year-old man was proud to have been remembered by the President. Proud that he might be useful to his country even yet, because he once had known France and Marshal Pétain so well. J.J.P. walked around the big table where the reporters had tossed their hats. His heels hit the polished black and white floor firmly. As he approached the door to his Commander in Chief's office, John Joseph Pershing thrust his shoulders back to full military *attention!* The little *click-click* of his heels was the only sound in the shadowy room.

The reporters had fallen silent. They watched the old man in the gray business suit advance "to answer his Last Command." Brecht thought that he almost could hear drums and see the flutter of ghostly battle flags going ahead of the old General. Then the door to the President's office opened, and Pershing disappeared through it.

Only then did anyone speak.

"Well, here we go again, boys," said a reporter quietly.

# Index

# Index